W9-CFQ-742

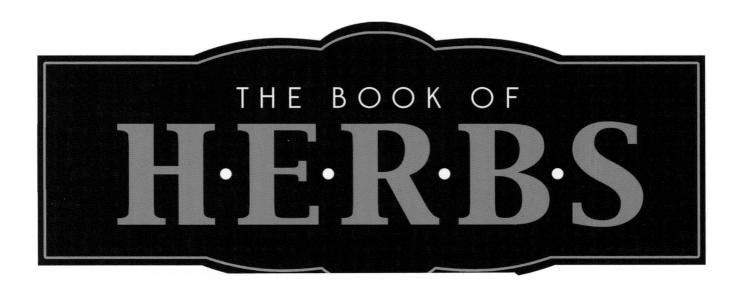

THE BOOK OF
H·E·R·B·S

Generously donated by

Dolores & William Redican

knowledge gives us wings

LONG BEACH PUBLIC LIBRARY

BARTY PHILLIPS

AN
ILLUSTRATED
A-Z OF THE
WORLD'S
MOST POPULAR
CULINARY AND
MEDICINAL PLANTS

THE BOOK OF
H·E·R·B·S

HOBBLE CREEK PRESS
AN IMPRINT OF CEDAR FORT, INC.
SPRINGVILLE, UTAH

This book is intended as a guide to herbs for food, health, and household. While every effort has been made to ensure this book contains warnings, where necessary, about the possible dangers of substances mentioned herein, it may be advisable to consult a qualified medical practitioner before use.

The publisher, the editor, and their respective employees shall not accept responsibility for injury, loss, or damage occasioned to any person acting or refraining from action as a result of material in this book, whether or not such injury, loss, or damage is in any way due to any negligent act or omission on the part of the publisher, editor, or their employees.

ISBN 13: 978-1-4621-1238-8

The US edition published in 2013 by Hobble Creek Press, an imprint of Cedar Fort, Inc.
2373 W. 700 S., Springville, UT, 84663
Distributed by Cedar Fort, Inc., www.cedarfort.com

Previous edition published in 2009 in England by Arcturus Publishing Limited

LIBRARY OF CONGRESS CATALOGING-IN-PUBLICATION DATA

Phillips, Barty.
 The book of herbs / Barty Phillips.
    pages cm
 Includes bibliographical references and index.
 ISBN 978-1-4621-1238-8 (alk. paper)
 1. Herbs. 2. Herbs--Thearapeutic use. 3. Cooking (Herbs) I. Title.
 SB351.H5P475 2013
 635'.7--dc23
                          2013000395

Cover design by Erica Dixon
Cover design © 2013 by Lyle Mortimer
Editing for the US edition by Casey J. Winters

Printed in the United States of America

10 9 8 7 6 5 4 3 2 1

CONTENTS

Clockwise from top left: black pepper, chives, mint, rosemary, oregano, feverfew.

INTRODUCTION

Herbs are nature's most useful plants. For centuries, they have been prized for their health-giving properties, and for their ability to add delicious flavors to food. Herbs were among the earliest plants to be cultivated, and their culinary, medical and cosmetic benefits have been studied since ancient times.

Now, *The Book of Herbs* brings together this wealth of information in one handy volume. It covers everything from everyday favorites, such as sage (used as a powerful soothing agent, as well as the perfect flavoring for rich meats), to more unusual plants like the tasty and nutritious Good King Henry, once one of Europe's most widely used culinary herbs.

Each page has a picture of the plant itself, with extra pictures explaining which parts are used and how to prepare them. Then there's a ready-reference panel that gives you a quick guide to the plant's properties. This is divided into sections covering the herb's culinary uses, medical benefits (including any special precautions), household and cosmetic applications. Finally, there's a panel that describes the plant in detail, including its history and cultivation—with advice on herbs you might want to grow yourself.

The pages are in alphabetical order, making it easy to find the herb you're interested in, or just browse to discover a wealth of fascinating new plant lore. And because some herbs are known by different common names, you'll find an index of all their botanical names at the back of the book.

ALOE VERA

This sun-loving plant will grow in dry conditions. It is cultivated commercially for the sap that can be extracted from its leaves. The sap is used for its healing and moisturizing properties.

Leaf
Thick, fleshy, tapering to a point. Pale green, often flecked with white, with small spines along edges.

The sap taken from the fleshy leaves of aloe vera has given this plant a reputation for almost miraculous soothing, healing, and moisturizing properties. Today, it appears as an ingredient in many creams, suntan lotions, and hair-care products.

The clear, gelatinous sap has a remarkable effect on burnt or irritated skin. It forms a soothing and protective barrier that allows the skin beneath to heal undisturbed. If aloe vera gel is applied to a burn immediately, it can prevent the formation of scar tissue. Aloe vera is so effective that it even has a reputation for healing radiation burns.

Strong Medicine
Aloes have been used medicinally for over two thousand years. An extract called "bitter aloes" is used as a laxative, and in some countries its use is subject to legal restrictions.

Aloe vera juice, which is now widely available in health food shops, is quite different from bitter aloes. It may help in cases of stubborn constipation since it has a soothing, possibly laxative effect on the bowel.

Origins
Aloe vera originates in tropical Africa, and Muslims regard the aloe as a religious symbol. In the past, those who had made the sacred pilgrimage to Mecca were entitled to hang the aloe over their doorway. Four hundred years ago, aloe vera was taken to the West Indies, where it is now widely cultivated on a commercial scale.

Leaf Base
Has no stem but a base from which leaves, and eventually a flowering spike, grow.

Root
Strong, due to ability to grow in scrubby land. Light brown and fibrous.

Split Leaf
Contains soothing gelatinous sap, used to heal burns and moisturize dry skin.

USES

PARTS USED:
Leaves.

PROPERTIES:
Soothing, healing, and moisturizing.

USES OF THE HERB:
Medicinal
Slice fresh leaves and apply to skin to ease dermatitis, eczema, or extreme dryness. Apply a little gel from a cut leaf to a small burn or open a leaf and bandage in place—gel side down—over a large burn, before seeking medical attention. Aloe vera gel can be applied directly to insect bites and fungal infections. Cut the leaf open and apply the gel directly to the afflicted part.

Cosmetic
Use the gel in homemade moisturizing creams, or use in shampoos for an itchy scalp. Used in aftersun lotion for its soothing properties.

CAUTION
Seek medical attention for severe burns. Avoid aloe vera in pregnancy. Some countries legally restrict the use of the purgative "bitter aloes."

ARNICA

This herb has a wide range of medicinal applications and has been used as a healing aid for many centuries. Today, however, its safety has been questioned in some countries. In the garden, this alpine plant is suitable for rock gardens and raised beds.

Arnica is one of the most famous plants in the herbal medicine cabinet. This aromatic and astringent herb stimulates the heart and immune system, and also acts as an anti-inflammatory and painkiller. It fights off bacterial and fungal infection and can be used externally for a wide range of conditions—most notably bruising, but also sprains, dislocations, chilblains, and varicose ulcers.

Cause of Controversy
In recent years, the safety of arnica remedies has been questioned, and they are now used only externally in the UK and are ruled unsafe in North America. In Germany and Austria, however, the dried flowers are still used commonly in a range of medicinal preparations. Arnica's most controversial application is as a short-term treatment for heart failure and coronary artery disease, but even used externally it can cause skin irritation. Homeopathic preparations aimed at speeding healing following an accident are regarded as safe.

Arnica Tea
The name "arnica" comes from the ancient Greek language, but its exact origins are uncertain. Some say it is derived from *arnakis*, meaning "lamb's skin," a reference to its soft leaves; others that it comes from *ptarmikos*, the Greek word for sneezing—one whiff of this aromatic herb can make you sneeze.

It was a staple household remedy in sixteenth-century Germany—the writer Goethe (1749–1832) was said to drink arnica tea to combat his angina—and it was later used in Italy too.

Alpine Climate
As *Arnica montana* is an alpine plant, it requires a cool, moist climate. It may do well in a rock garden or other area of raised ground. It is restricted by law in many countries—regulations should be checked before gathering it from the wild.

USES

PARTS USED:
Flowers.

PROPERTIES:
Astringent, stimulates heart and immune system, relieves pain, anti-inflammatory, combats bacterial and fungal infection.

USES OF THE HERB:
Medicinal
Taken internally for heart failure and coronary artery disease; externally for bruises, sprains, dislocations, chilblains, varicose ulcers, throat gargle. In homeopathy for epilepsy, sea sickness, and salmonella, and to encourage hair growth.

CAUTION
Toxic—for expert use only. Prescribed externally only in the UK and ruled unsafe in North America. May irritate skin—never apply to broken skin.

Flower
Golden, daisy-like flowers.

Leaf
Soft, oval-shaped, and covered in fine hairs. Up to 7 in. long. Arranged in a rosette around the stem base.

BASIL

No other herb stands out quite like basil for its aroma—shred its leaves and the pungent smell fills the air, and it has a flavor to match.

Basil, also known as "sweet basil," is one of the world's major culinary herbs, and its aromatic leaves are well known for the seasoning they bring to many dishes. Originally from India, the herb has long been cultivated throughout Europe and the Mediterranean. It is particularly important in Italian cooking; it is a main ingredient of pesto sauce and tastes delicious with tomatoes, garlic, and aubergines. It also suits shellfish and can be added to omelets. Basil flavors soups and sauces and is used to make flavored oils and marinades or basil vinegar. It is rich in vitamin A, vitamin C, calcium, and iron. Fresh basil is readily available to almost everyone since it can be raised in pots indoors.

Herb Tonic

Basil has an uplifting effect on the nervous system. The essential oil is often used in aromatherapy to treat depression and negativity. Because it can also ease overworked and stressed muscles, basil is popular with dancers and athletes. Basil is good for the digestive system. An infusion of the fresh leaves will help nervous dyspepsia, or you can chew on a small leaf to ease indigestion or flatulence. The tea is said to relieve nausea.

In the Garden

There are over one hundred sixty varieties of basil worldwide. Some can look very attractive outside in the herb garden, and different varieties can look appealing when grown side by side. The purple leaves of the Dark Opal or Purple Ruffle varieties are an excellent counterpart to the usual green. To add to the scent of the garden, lemon basil (*Ocimum basilicum* var *citriodorum*) is a good choice. Although many insects are repelled by basil, it attracts butterflies and bees. In its native India, basil was considered sacred, second only to the lotus flower. And in other countries too it has the reputation of being a sacred herb. It was reputedly found growing around Christ's tomb after the resurrection, so in some Greek Orthodox churches, it is used to prepare holy water, and pots of basil are often set below the altar and at the foot of the pulpit.

USES

PARTS USED:
Leaves, stems, and flowers.

PROPERTIES:
Contains vitamins A and C and calcium and iron; the essential oil is uplifting.

USES OF THE HERB:
Culinary
Traditionally, basil should be torn with the fingers rather than chopped. It tastes delicious sprinkled over salads and is an important part of many sauces.

Medicinal
Make tea by pouring a cup of boiling water over three teaspoons of basil leaves as a remedy for colds, flu, catarrh, and digestive upsets. (Do not take basil medicinally if you are pregnant.)

Household
Pots of basil in the kitchen will keep flies away. A fresh leaf rubbed on an insect bite will help lessen the irritation.

CAUTION
Therapeutic doses of basil should not be used in pregnancy.

Basil
Leafy, aromatic herb rich in a complex mixture of aromatic oils. ' "Genovese," one of many variants of this widely grown plant, favored for Italian dishes, grows to about 18 in.

Dried Leaf
Can be crushed for use in cooking, or in potpourri. Infuse instead of fresh leaves as a tea that aids digestion and soothes respiratory problems.

Greek Basil
A miniature variant, also called "bush basil." Has a compact growth and very small leaves. Flavor is not so strong as some of the larger-leafed varieties.

BAY

The history of bay is well documented—the ancient Greeks crowned their athletes with wreaths of it, the Romans used it as a symbol of wisdom, and the French cooked with it.

Also known as sweet bay or bay laurel, the dried leaves of this herb tree are used as a seasoning in sweet and savory cooking all over the world. Today, the essential oil is widely used in commercial condiments, sauces, and meat products.

Tree of the Gods
In ancient times, bay was sacred to the gods. The roof of Apollo's temple at Delphi was entirely made of its leaves. Bay was also dedicated to the god of medicine and for centuries was used to ward off disease, especially in times of plague, when it was strewn around the house. A bay wreath became a mark of excellence for athletes and poets, and the Romans used it as a symbol of wisdom. The Latin for "crowned with laurel" survives in the modern "poet laureate," while the laurel wreath appears on sports trophies to this day.

Ancient Healer
The tree has always served a decorative purpose and thrives on being clipped. Since the sixteenth century, bushes have been carefully trained into ornamental shapes. One traditional design is the "ball bay," which is trimmed to a globe at the top of a smooth, bare trunk. This is the traditional tree often seen on patios or beside entrances.

The bay tree is one of two small shrubs or evergreen trees in this genus. It is native to the Mediterranean region and likes full sun—although it tolerates partial shade—and a rich soil. In colder climates, clipped bushes are best grown in a tub so that they can be moved to a sheltered spot or indoors during winter. It is best grown from cuttings.

USES

PARTS USED:
Leaves.

PROPERTIES:
Aromatic, culinary flavoring.

USES OF THE HERB:
Culinary
Use bay leaves as part of a bouquet garni for soups, stews, and sauces. Add to stocks, marinades and stews, curry, and poached fish. Remove leaves before serving. Place in rice jar to flavor rice. Heat in milk to flavor custards and puddings. Use to flavor vinegar.

Medicinal
Use an infusion of the leaves as a digestive stimulant. Apply infusion to scalp to relieve dandruff. Essential oil is good for massaging sprains and rheumatic pains. Make sure the oil is diluted by mixing it with a "carrier oil" such as sweet almond beforehand.

Cosmetic
Add a decoction of bay to bath water to tone the skin and relieve aches.

Decorative
Clipped and trained bay trees in tubs are an elegant and traditional decoration for doorways and house walls. Use branches in full leaf for wreaths.

Household
Crumble dried leaves into potpourri. Hang branches up to freshen the air.

Dried Leaf
Like fresh leaves, can be used to flavor sauces, marinades, and so on. Use freshly dried because flavor fades.

Leaf
Aromatic, leathery, and shiny dark green with clear veining.

Stem
Young stems are purple-brown, becoming woody and gray with age.

11

Leaves
Oval leaves are dark green
with purplish tinge. Can
be dried for use in
potpourri.

BERGAMOT

The aromatic leaves and edible flowers of bergamot can be used for flavoring and decorating food. The plant also dries well, with the flowers retaining some of their color.

This North American woodland herb became a popular garden plant in Europe after explorers sent back the seeds. After the Boston Tea Party in 1773, when rioting settlers threw several hundred chests of Indian tea into the harbor, bergamot was used to make a substitute tea known as Oswego tea. Bergamot's Latin name, *Monarda*, recalls the Spanish botanist Dr. Nicholas Monardes, who wrote a book about the plants of America in 1569. He named this herb "bergamot" because the scent of its leaves resembles the Italian Bergamot orange (*Citrus bergamia*) from which an essential oil is made.

The bergamot plant usually has vivid scarlet flowers, although there are varieties that bear pink, purple, mauve, and white blooms. Hummingbirds are attracted to the flowers, and any garden featuring bergamot will attract more than its fair share of butterflies and bees. This gives rise to another popular name for bergamot—"bee balm."

Garden Beauty
The plant has claw-shaped, tubular flowers that bloom from July until September, when they can be harvested whole and preserved. The leaves of the plant are strongly aromatic (the aroma is strongest when the plant is young). This makes bergamot a good choice for planting along paths. As people brush past, it releases a delicious scent.

The edible flowers can be used to decorate salads. The leaves have a strong flavor and can be used sparingly in salads and stuffings. Dried leaves can be infused in water or milk. Native Americans used bergamot for chest and throat complaints.

Stem
Hard, dark green, and hairy,
with purplish tinge where
leaves join.

Seeds
Small dark-brown seeds
can be collected for sowing.

USES

PARTS USED:
Leaves and flowers.

PROPERTIES:
Aromatic.

USES OF THE HERB:
Decorative
Use in flower arrangements or to add scent and color to potpourri mixtures.

Culinary
Add the leaves to fruit salad and use the flowers to decorate puddings. Leaves can also be added to homemade lemonade to enhance the flavor. Add flowers to salads.

Medicinal
Drink an infusion for minor digestive complaints.

Household
Attracts a host of butterflies and bees to the garden.

BLACK PEPPER

The ancient Greeks and Romans used pepper as a condiment and a medicine. Later, it was a trading currency along the spice route. Today it is the most widely used spice in the world.

The familiar condiment that appears in kitchens and on dining tables all over the world—in either a black or white form, whole, ground, or powdered—comes from the pungent fruit of a tropical, climbing plant. The vine, *Piper nigrum*, is a glossy-leaved species whose small, aromatic berry-fruits are sun-dried when green and immature to form black peppercorns. Fruits that are left to ripen and are then dried before their outer layers are removed form white peppercorns, which have a less aromatic taste than their black counterparts. Peppercorns are also picked when green and are preserved in various ways for use where a milder spice is preferred. Pink peppercorns actually come from a different species and have been thought to be slightly toxic. There is also no connection with the glossy pepper fruits, including salad peppers and the many varieties of chillies, that belong to the genus *Capsicum*.

Ancient Spice

Native to Asia, especially India, Malaysia, and Indonesia, this is one of the oldest known spices in the world, used as a medicine and condiment in the times of the Greek physician Hippocrates. Pepper formed a vital trading commodity along the ancient spice routes and, later, across the vast trading sea routes traversed by European explorers. The term "peppercorn rent" comes from its value as a trading currency.

Worldwide Favor

Today pepper is no less valued, in every type of cuisine, around the world. It can be added to a vast range of savory dishes, and the warming and revitalizing properties of black pepper have been put to good use in both Western and Eastern medicine as well as in aromatherapy. This stimulating expectorant can be particularly effective in treating indigestion, gas, colds, and congestion, and is especially pleasant mixed with rose extracts. This is a species that demands tropical conditions. It can be cultivated, but not for its fruits, in a greenhouse or across a trellis.

USES

PARTS USED:
Berries.

PROPERTIES:
Aromatic, stimulant, expectorant.

USES OF THE HERB:
Culinary
Traditionally used ground and whole, dried, and fresh (green) in all kinds of savory dishes; ground black pepper on sliced strawberries and black pepper cookies is an unusually sweet treat. Whole peppercorns can be infused when making sauces, and a mild green fresh peppercorn sauce or coating complements rich meat and fish dishes.

Medicinal
Black pepper is used in aromatherapy to revitalize, while this warming stimulant and expectorant, with antiseptic properties, can help colds and sinusitis, nausea, indigestion, gas, and food poisoning.

Household
Ground or powdered pepper makes a natural deterrent in the house or garden for unwanted mice, cats, and dogs.

Stem
Twining, flexible stems.

Fruit
Berry-like fruits are pungently fragrant and wrinkled.

Leaves
Glossy, oval, dark leaves have conspicuous veining.

Peppercorns
The berries are green when immature and red when ripe.

Pepper Mill
An airtight pepper mill provides the best way to retain the flavor of dried peppercorns until they are needed. Most are adjustable for fine or coarse grinding.

BLUEBERRY

This shrub is widely cultivated commercially for its berries, which are a culinary favorite. The berries and leaves also have medicinal applications, including the treatment of skin problems.

Fruit
Sweet-tasting, blue-black berries with grayish sheen; ripen in late summer.

Blueberries belong to the same family as bilberries (*Vaccinium myrtillus*) and share many of the same culinary and medicinal uses. Delicious to eat when freshly picked, they will keep in the refrigerator for several days and feature in many favorite recipes—including blueberry cheesecake, blueberry muffins, and blueberry pancakes. These berries are perfect for syrups or jam-making, requiring less added sugar than many other fruits—adding a dash of lemon or lime juice gives them a sharper taste. They can also be added to thick yogurt.

Berry Benefits
Like bilberries, blueberries are astringent and cooling, with a diuretic effect (and laxative in large quantities). Blueberry preparations can lower blood sugar levels and are taken for diabetes as well as for edema, anemia, urinary complaints, dysentery, diarrhea, and intestinal problems in general. Applied externally, a decoction of the fruit also soothes hemorrhoids, burns, eczema, and other skin ailments, and makes a good gargle or mouthwash for inflamed gums. The juice is said to soothe inflamed eyes. Extracts are rich in anthocyanidins and are taken as supplements to maintain health of peripheral circulation and skin collagen. Bilberries were known to the ancient Greek physician Dioscorides, who recommended them for stomach upsets and intestinal problems. The juice became a folk remedy for improving night vision. The berries were once commonly prescribed for dropsy and scurvy—a condition caused by chronic shortage of vitamin C, often suffered by sailors. The fruit also yields a dark-blue or purple dye.

Mass Cultivation
Highbush blueberries, derived from *Vaccinium corymbosum*, are the preferred crop for mass commercial cultivation, and rabbit-eye blueberries (*Vaccinium ashei*) are also important economically.

Stem
Many hairless branches, short and stiff, up to 24 in. in height.

Leaf
Bright green, egg-shaped leaves with short stalks and toothed margins.

Berries
The color of the berries (fruit) changes as they ripen.

USES

PARTS USED:
Leaves, fruits.

PROPERTIES:
Astringent, cooling, diuretic, laxative, lowers blood sugar, and has a tonic effect on the blood.

USES OF THE HERB:
Medicinal
Taken internally for diabetes (leaves), anemia, edema, dysentery, diarrhea and urinary problems. Applied to hemorrhoids, burns (fruit), eczema, and other skin complaints. Made into mouthwash for inflamed gums. Soothes sore eyes. Proven to combat typhoid and bacilli of the colon. Extracts maintain peripheral circulation (fine blood vessels) and skin collagen.

Culinary
Fruit is delicious fresh or made into jam, pies, puddings, syrups, cheesecake, muffins, or pancakes.

BORAGE

This attractive herb with its colorful flowers looks good in a perennial border and can be put to good use in the kitchen.

Borage is an attractive, flowering plant with a wide range of culinary and medicinal uses. It is traditionally reputed to bestow both courage and happiness—the Celtic word *borrach* means courage. In ancient times, borage was used to make herbal wine, which the ancient Greek poet Homer is supposed to have called the wine of forgetfulness. In medieval England, borage flowers were floated on the stirrup-cups given to departing Crusader knights.

Borage flowers are edible, as are borage leaves, which have a cucumber flavor. They are normally a vividly bright blue color and often appear in illustrated medieval texts and tapestries. The plants may sometimes produce pink or white flowers. Once dried, borage flowers make an ideal addition to potpourri.

Traditionally, the herb is well known for its ability to calm anxiety and nervous disorders. Recent medical research has shown that borage's high concentrations of minerals and complex compounds may work on the adrenal glands and have a stimulating effect similar to that of adrenaline, the source of courage.

Native Roots

Originally a native of the Mediterranean and western Asia, and often found growing on wasteland and rough ground, this herb thrives best on rich, moist, well-drained soil. The plants tend to have a long, robust taproot, which means that transplanting is seldom successful and growing in pots or containers is not generally advised. The best situations for this plant are herb gardens or perennial borders. However, a few seeds can be sown to produce small plants for winter use, as long as they are kept indoors in a light, warm spot.

USES

PARTS USED:
Leaves, flowers, seeds, oil.

PROPERTIES:
Cooling, saline, diuretic; mildly sedative and antidepressant.

USES OF THE HERB:
Culinary
Use flowers in salads as a garnish or crystallize for cake decorations. Add young leaves to summer drinks. Chop leaves to use in ravioli stuffing.

Medicinal
Use leaves in a poultice to soothe bruises. Seed oil may be effective in treating premenstrual tension and lowering blood pressure.

Cosmetic
Add leaves to a face pack for dry skin or mix with barley and use in bath bags.

Household
Flowers attract bees to gardens. When planted near tomatoes, helps to control tomato worm.

CAUTION
May irritate the skin or cause allergies. All members of the borage family are restricted in some countries for medicinal use because they may cause liver damage.

Leaf
Although covered with prickly hairs, leaves are edible, with medicinal and cosmetic uses.

Stem
Sturdy, round stems are hollow and hairy.

Seeds
Large, dark brown seeds remain viable for several years. Contain starflower oil that has medicinal uses.

Leaf
Shiny and pointed, up to 4 in. long. Red when young, with a strong camphor aroma.

CAMPHOR

This evergreen tree is economically important—extracts are used in various ways, including in the manufacture of mothballs. It is also featured in traditional Oriental medicines.

The pungent, aromatic oil, which has numerous uses, makes camphor one of the world's most valuable trees. The wood is boiled to extract crystallized camphor, which is used to make mothballs or mixed with peanut oil to make camphorated oil. The oil treats a wide range of health problems, and it is used in the manufacture of celluloid (film).

Cancer Risk
The oil also contains a substance called "safrole." Once used to flavor food, this is now banned in many countries because of suggestions that it may cause cancer. Camphor is toxic in excess, and camphorated oil is subject to legal restrictions as a medication in some countries. It can cause sickness, palpitations, convulsions, and, ultimately, death; it is particularly dangerous because it can be absorbed through the skin.

Healing Aroma
Camphor is often applied externally in liniments or balms to ease joint and muscular pains, chilblains, cold sores, and chapped lips. It may be inhaled as a decongestant and is prescribed in traditional Chinese medicine (known as *zhang nao*) for wounds and skin diseases, and to revive an unconscious patient. Aromatherapists use camphor to treat digestive problems and depression, while it is taken internally in ayurvedic medicine for asthma, bronchitis, sinusitis, eye complaints, epilepsy, gout, menstrual pain, rheumatism, and insomnia.

Embalming Aid
Camphor was used in China to embalm the dead and also to make varnish and Chinese inks. It is one of many Cinnamomum species with an interesting range of uses—others include *Cinnamomum cassia* (cassia bark), recorded in China around 2700 BC, and *C. zeylanicum*, a major spice from Sri Lanka and southern India. Compounds very similar to those in camphor oil are found in Ngai camphor (*Blumea balsamifera*) and in Borneo camphor (*Dryobalanops aromatica*). The latter plays a part in funeral ceremonies in Borneo and Sumatra.

Stem
Smooth, pale green. Trunk reaches 100 ft. in height. Wood boiled to extract crystallized oil of camphor.

Camphor Oil
Pungent, aromatic, and yellowy in color—is produced in the nooks and crannies of the tree's trunk.

USES

PARTS USED:
Leaves, wood, oil.

PROPERTIES:
Stimulates the nervous system and circulation, anti-inflammatory, relieves pain, aids digestion, and kills parasites.

USES OF THE HERB:
Medicinal
Important in Chinese medicine (wood and leaves known as *zhang nao*)—applied externally in liniments for joint and muscular pain, chilblains, chapped lips, cold sores, wounds, and skin problems. Inhaled to clear congestion and used in aromatherapy for depression. Used in ayurvedic medicine for bronchitis, asthma, sinusitis, epilepsy, menstrual pain, gout, rheumatism, and insomnia.

CAUTION
Poisonous in excess; can be absorbed through the skin. Causes sickness, palpitations, convulsions, death. Controlled by law as a medication in some countries.

CAPER BUSH

Enjoyed by the ancient Greeks and Romans, capers are still popular today as a flavoring ingredient and condiment. The plant is used to treat ailments such as gout and flatulence.

Stem
Long, trailing stems.

Basking in the hot Mediterranean sun, wild specimens of this sprawling shrub are often seen draped over coastal rocks or springing from rocky crevices. With its slightly fleshy leaves and purple-stamened blooms, *Capparis spinosa* is grown as an ornamental, and it is commercially cultivated on a large scale for its most famous product—the condiment known as capers. Capers are actually the pickled flower buds of this spiny perennial shrub. When the buds are young, firm, and unopened, they are pickled in either salt or a mixture of vinegar and salt. This pickling brings out the unique peppery and piquant taste of the buds, which contain a kind of mustard oil. Capers should be kept in their pickling medium or they will rapidly lose their flavor.

Flower
Single, four-petalled flowers, white or pink. Distinctive, long, purple-pink stamens. Edible capers are young pickled flower buds.

Sharp Note
Capers add a sharp, salty note to all kinds of dishes—pasta, pizzas, salads, vegetables, and meat, poultry, and fish recipes. They are delicious in all kinds of sauces. Capers are mixed with sardines in a well-known Italian pasta dish and are extremely popular in Provence—the paste known as "tapenade," a tasty mix of olives, capers, and anchovies, takes its name from *tapéno*, the Provençal word for capers.

Medicinal Uses
The buds and root-bark of this stimulating plant also have their medicinal uses, easing ailments as diverse as gout and flatulence. They also contain the antioxidant bioflavonoid rutin. There has been talk of the plant's use for skin problems, but it seems that it may be an irritant.

Persian Origins
Capers have been enjoyed in Mediterranean countries since the ancient Romans and Greeks. The genus name comes from a Persian word for caper, *kabar*. Today, capers are gathered from both wild and cultivated shrubs, and the latter are usually spineless.

Leaf
Slightly fleshy, oval, and alternate; two spines at base.

USES

PARTS USED
Root bark and flower buds.

PROPERTIES:
Astringent, bitter, diuretic, and expectorant; stimulating tonic.

USES OF THE HERB:
Medicinal
Aid stomach upsets, kidney infections, diarrhea, coughs, edema, anemia, rheumatism, arthritis, and gout, and help expel worms. Used in ayurvedic medicine as a liver tonic. External application for eye infections.

Culinary
Peppery, piquant capers used in hors d'oeuvres, sauces, pizzas, salads, and all kinds of meat, fish (especially salmon), and chicken dishes. Add an unusual, sharp note to vegetables. An ingredient of tapenade paste. For an unusual flavor, preserve capers in olive oil. Young leafy shoots and semi-ripe fruits (caperberries) can also be pickled and used as capers, or eaten as a vegetable.

CAUTION
May be a skin irritant.

Fruit
Also known as caperberries; semi-ripe fruits can be pickled and used in place of the flower buds.

Leaf
Fine, feathery leaves are
bright green in color.

CARAWAY

The seeds of this plant are a familiar culinary
ingredient, but the leaves and roots also lend
themselves to various uses.

The caraway plant is known best for its small, aromatic seeds, which
can be used in all kinds of culinary, medicinal, and decorative ways.
The seeds of the caraway plant have a long, cosmopolitan history and
have been found along the famed Silk Road—the ancient trade route
linking eastern China with Asia and Europe. The name "caraway" actually comes from the Arabic word for these seeds—*karawya*. Today
the plant is found across much of Europe, Asia, and North Africa, and
naturally tends to favor upland pastures and footpaths.

Cumin and Anise
With a spicy flavor somewhere between cumin and anise, the fresh
leaves of the caraway plant are added to salads and soups, while the
roots can be prepared and eaten like other root vegetables. As for the
major culinary part of the plant—its aromatic seeds—these are added
to all kinds of cooked fruit dishes and are used to flavor cakes, breads,
cookies, and candy. They are also used in certain hard cheeses. The
seeds are also popular in eastern European cuisine—they are added
to cabbage and goulash recipes, and rye bread. They can also be
included in a dish of mixed seeds to accompany Indian food.

Medicinally, this stimulant, expectorant herb promotes a healthy
digestive system and can ease bronchitis by encouraging coughing.
The oil extracted from the plant is used as a flavoring and in perfume.

Distinguished Connections
The caraway plant has a long and distinguished history. Seeds have
been uncovered at Stone Age sites and were used in the Middle East
for many thousands of years. They were also extremely popular during
medieval and Elizabethan times. According to country lore, caraway
was an herb to be used in love potions, as it was said to promote
constancy. The herb is easy to grow and will self-seed enthusiasti-
cally—some seed heads should be left on the plant.

Stem
Slender, hairless, hollow,
and ridged.

Seeds
The seeds have culinary and medicinal
uses and are widely used as a flavoring
ingredient.

USES

PARTS USED:
Leaves, roots, seeds, and oil.

PROPERTIES:
**Aromatic stimulant; reduces uterine
and gastrointestinal spasms; promotes productive coughing.**

USES OF THE HERB:
Culinary
**Add leaves to salads and soups,
and seeds to vegetable dishes, meat
stews, cooked fruits, cheese, and
baked foods.**

Medicinal
**Chewing seeds or taking seed infu-
sions eases indigestion, boosts the
appetite, and helps stomach ulcers
and diarrhea. Infusions help bronchitis and menstrual pain.**

Cosmetic
**Chew seeds as a quick breath-
freshener.**

Decorative
**The dried, tan-colored seed heads
are attractive in arrangements.**

CAUTION
**This can be confused with certain
poisonous species, so only use
specimens homegrown from seed.**

CARDAMOM

This is probably one of the most exotic and aromatic of herbs. It comes from the Far East and is used in sweet and savory foods and in medicine, and its oil is used in cosmetics.

Cardamom is one of the herbs that truly conjures up images of the exotic, and it has been exported from its home in the rainforests of India for thousands of years. Its seeds have an aroma rather like that of eucalyptus and originally became valuable for their essential oil, prized by perfume-makers.

The seeds are also a common feature of Indian pickles, curries, and desserts, and are often used ground, although they soon lose their strong flavor once in powder form. The seeds are also used to flavor novelty breads and other baked goods in northern Europe.

Ayurvedic Remedy
Elettaria cardamomum is one of the key herbs in ayurvedic medicine, usually prescribed for bronchial ailments or poor digestion—particularly in the case of dairy products, which can trigger excessive mucus formation in some people.

A stimulating tonic with expectorant and antispasmodic properties, cardamom is taken for nausea and vomiting, urinary incontinence, and various kinds of lung and kidney disease. Seeds from the small green fruit are known in Chinese medicine as *sha ren* and are associated with kidney dysfunction, while the larger white fruits are more often prescribed for lung ailments.

Caravan Route
Cardamom arrived in Europe from the East in classical times, via the ancient caravan trading routes. It was first recorded in Chinese medicine around the year AD 720. There are a number of varieties of *E. cardamomum*, but only seeds from the true species possess the characteristic aroma and taste, while those of related species tend to smell slightly camphoraceous.

USES

PARTS USED:
Seeds, oil.

PROPERTIES:
Warming, stimulating, tonic, expectorant, antispasmodic, and improves digestion.

USES OF THE HERB:
Medicinal
Aids digestion—especially of mucus-forming foods such as dairy products. Good for lungs and kidneys. Taken internally for nausea and vomiting, urinary incontinence, and lung disease with phlegm. Prescribed in ayurvedic medicine for bronchial and digestive problems.

Culinary
Seeds flavor curries and pickles, baked goods, fruit compotes, and milky desserts.

Cosmetic
Essential oil used in perfumery.

Leaf
Spear-shaped leaves up to 2 ft. in length.

Stem
Tall, cane-like stems.

Seed Pods
Seeds from small green fruits have culinary and medicinal uses.

Leaf
Soft, heart-shaped, and hairy leaves have a distinctly toothed edge and release a strong, minty fragrance when crushed.

CATMINT

Apart from being a feline favorite, this plant has a range of medicinal applications, notably to treat fevers. It is also used to make an herbal tea and the French use it as a flavoring.

Irresistibly drawn to the minty aroma released when the leaves of this species are crushed, cats love to chew and roll around in these plants, giving rise to the traditional common name. Other common names for this plant include "catnip" and "catnep." It is thought that cats enjoy the stimulant effect of one particular constituent—a glycoside called "actinidine."

Traditionally a wild species of hedgerows, field edges, and waste ground across much of Europe, Asia, and North America, catmint is a bitter, cooling herb. Medicinally, it plays a soothing role and is valued for its ability to increase perspiration without raising the body's temperature. A tisane of the soft, gray-green leaves or flowering tops quiets fevers, especially those associated with colds and flu, and acts as a natural tranquilizer, calming conditions such as nervous tension, indigestion, and insomnia. The French are especially fond of using the leaves of this plant as a flavoring ingredient in certain dishes. The dried minty leaves are also suitable to be used as a stuffing for cat toys.

Stimulating Properties
Catmint tea is a traditional country tonic, thanks to its generally stimulating nature. One story tells of a hangman who was unable to discharge his duties until he had gained courage from a cup of a brew made out of catmint.

Easy to grow in most types of soil, as long as the ground is well drained and kept free of weeds, catmint will thrive if compost is added in spring and dead stems are cut back in autumn. The plant flowers around August and should last for a few years. It is generally thought that sowing seeds is a better propagation option than transplanting, as cats will detect the aroma of small plants and may destroy them.

Garden Choices
Catmint plants make an attractive feature in perennial and mixed borders, although certain other *Nepeta* plants have brighter coloring and are more obvious choices as garden ornamentals. These species—also referred to as catnip—tend to be less potent when it comes to attracting cats.

USES

PARTS USED:
Whole plant, leaves.

PROPERTIES:
Astringent, bitter, cooling herb; camphoraceous aroma.

USES OF THE HERB:
Culinary
The mint-like leaves make a pleasant tea—especially those of the lemony cultivar N. cataria "Citriodora." Use as a mint substitute or add young shoots to salads.

Medicinal
Drinking leaf-infusions relieves colds, fevers, and indigestion. Its calming effect helps nervousness, nervous stomach upsets, head-aches, and sleeplessness. External poultices reduce inflammation and swelling.

Cosmetic
Makes a cleansing hair wash.

Household
Dried leaves are used to stuff cat toys.

Stem
Square-shaped, mint-scented stem covered with fine hairs.

Seeds
Each seed case encloses four oval seeds, dark brown with white ends. The seeds are viable for about five years.

CHERVIL

Chervil has been used for its medicinal and culinary properties for many centuries. It also makes an attractive garden plant and is suitable for mixed borders and containers.

This delicately aromatic herb is a perfect choice for garden containers. Enjoyed fresh, in large quantities, this staple of French cuisine adds a subtle, slightly bitter aniseed flavor to a wide range of meat and vegetable dishes. It is the leaves that are usually used, although the stem can be chopped and used in stews and casseroles. It is best used fresh because it doesn't retain its flavor well when dried. The *Anthriscus* genus to which chervil belongs contains annuals, biennials, and perennials, from Europe, north Africa, and Asia. Chervil is a leafy biennial which has become increasingly popular as a culinary plant in recent years.

Ancient Cure

The medicinal value of chervil was praised as far back as the days of ancient Rome. The herb's therapeutic uses revolve around its cleansing and expectorant properties. It can be used to ease fluid retention and relieve liver and kidney problems. It will also aid the smooth functioning of the digestive system. Other health conditions that respond to chervil include conjunctivitis, swollen eyelids, and hemorrhoids, where chervil preparations are applied externally, and jaundice, rheumatism, and eczema, when taken internally. The leaves are also a source of vitamins and minerals—vitamin C, carotene, magnesium, and iron.

The chervil plant has a delicate, slender stem and fine, feathery leaves that take on a faint pink-purple hue during the last weeks of summer. Tiny white flowers, arranged in little clusters, appear during the late summer months. For the best result, chervil plants should be positioned in a moist, shady spot. Country lore claims that planting the herb next to radishes will give the radishes a much hotter flavor.

A fresh supply of leaves can be kept going through the warmer months by sowing seeds every few weeks through spring and summer. To keep a fresh supply going through the winter months, seeds should be sown in autumn and plants raised under protection.

USES

PARTS USED:
Stems and leaves.

PROPERTIES:
A cleansing expectorant containing vitamins and minerals.

USES OF THE HERB:
Culinary
Add to salads and fish, chicken, egg, and potato dishes, as well as soups and sauces. Cooking and drying destroys the subtle flavor, so use large quantities of fresh leaves, toward the end of cooking times. Chervil brings out the flavor of some other herbs very well—try cooking fish with a combination of chervil and lemon balm.

Medicinal
The herb's tonic, expectorant properties aid digestive and urinary functions—take a cup of chervil tea to cleanse the system.

Cosmetic
A chervil face mask cleanses and softens skin, while a poultice on closed eyelids refreshes tired eyes.

Stem
Delicate stem is hollow and ridged and can be chopped and added to various dishes.

Leaf
Lacy, bright green leaf that resembles Italian parsley and has a hint of its flavor.

Dried Chervil
Drying chervil destroys its subtle flavor for culinary purposes, but the dried leaves are used medicinally.

Seeds
Long, thin seeds, dark in color.

CHICORY

Cultivated as a vegetable since Roman times, chicory, despite its bitterness, has a long history of culinary and medicinal uses. It has been used to treat liver complaints and as a general tonic.

Chicory grows wild in Europe and other parts of the world. It is one of the best-known plants in the herb garden. *Cichorium intybus* is related to the endive, *C. endivia*. This often causes confusion because in some countries, curly endive is called "French chichorée," while pale-colored chicory is known as "endive."

Three Main Types

There are three basic kinds of leaf chicory. First, the bitter, loose-leaved cultivars grown as a winter vegetable in southern Italy and other regions. Second, the white Belgian witloof type, with narrower leaves and a head called a chicon, which can be added to salads or braised in butter. Third, there are the red, radicchio types, with larger leaves and cabbage-like heads. Roasted chicory roots have a caramel taste. Other chicories include *pain de sucre* (sugar loaf), which resembles lettuce, and red verona, another good salad ingredient with crimson leaves.

Gallstone Remedy

Chicory features in many folk tales, reflecting its importance as a medicinal as well as culinary herb. The alternative name, "succory," probably comes from the Latin verb *succurrere*, meaning "to run under," reflecting the deep-reaching roots.

Chicory is diuretic, laxative, and anti-inflammatory, and is still taken today for liver complaints, rheumatism, gout, hemorrhoids, and gallstones. Practitioners of ayurvedic medicine prescribe it for its cooling properties and as a general tonic. Chicory flowers were once distilled in water to soothe inflamed eyes or restore ailing sight, while the leaves were boiled to produce a blue dye, and the plant was grown as animal fodder. Today chicory is sometimes cultivated simply to brighten up a garden border with its sky-blue flowers, which open and close at fixed times of the day.

Flower
Clusters of sky-blue flowers (sometimes pink or white), similar to dandelions and appealing to bumblebees.

Leaf
Large, hairy, coarsely toothed leaves, arranged in a basal rosette.

Stem
Stiff, branching stem.

Chicory Roots
Chicory roots have been ground and roasted since the seventeenth century as a coffee substitute or additive.

USES

PARTS USED:
Leaves, roots.

PROPERTIES:
Bitter, diuretic, laxative; tonic effect on gallbladder; anti-inflammatory.

USES OF THE HERB:
Medicinal
Dried roots are diuretic, laxative, anti-inflammatory, and stimulating to the liver and gallbladder. Prescribed for rheumatism, gout, and hemorrhoids, and as a general tonic.

Culinary
Young leaves and flowers added to salads. Blanch and cook in various different ways; whole heads delicious braised slowly in butter and served with a white or cheese sauce. Roots can also be eaten while young and tender, or roasted as a coffee substitute.

CHIVES

Chives are related to onion and garlic, all of which are members of the *Allium* genus. Most alliums are popular for both their culinary uses and health-giving properties.

The familiar chives variety (*Allium schoenoprasum*) has pretty, pale purple flowers, and hollow, cylindrical leaves that taper to a fine point. The leaves, which are the most commonly used part of the plant, have a mild onion-like flavor that is excellent for seasoning a wide range of dishes, especially when onion itself is too strong.

While chives are not really used as a medicinal herb, their leaves contain very large amounts of vitamins A and C along with other minerals and vitamins.

Growing Chives
Chives look delightful as an edging plant, or in window boxes and pots. But when chives are being grown primarily for cooking, rather than decoration, the flowers should be removed to prevent the plant from becoming exhausted—they can be used to great effect in a range of salads. Chives should be cut very low after flowering in order to produce fresh leaves. The leaves are best snipped or chopped and used fresh as required. Fresh leaves can be used in salads, soups, and sandwiches, as a garnish, or to flavor butter or soft cheeses. Chives do not dry particularly well, and dried leaves are best used in cooked dishes.

Chinese Chives
Another variety, Chinese chives (*Allium tuberosum*), has a mild garlic flavor that may be enjoyed by those who prefer a less pungent form of garlic. Their use was first recorded four thousand years ago in China, and they were appreciated by the famous traveller Marco Polo, who helped to popularize them in the West. Medicinally they are said to improve kidney function. Chinese chives can also be grown with ease. They have clusters of starry white flowers.

USES

PARTS USED:
Leaves and flowers.

PROPERTIES:
Contains vitamins A and C and minerals.

USES OF THE HERB:
Culinary
Sprinkle florets or cut leaves on salads, in sandwiches, and in soups, and use generally as a garnish. Chives can be delicious when added to either butter or cream cheese and are especially good with potatoes and eggs. The chopped leaves are an essential ingredient of the chilled soup known as vichyssoise and are used in rémoulade. Dried chives can be reconstituted with lemon juice.

Medicinal
Fresh leaves and flowers are a mild aid to digestion. Alliums are often good for the blood vessels, keeping them elastic and helping to deter premature aging.

Household
An infusion of chives makes a spray that will remove aphids and mildew from garden plants.

Foliage
The leaves are long, grassy, and tubular. The color varies from medium to dark green.

Flowers
Chives are sometimes grown for the decorative purple florets that appear in summer. These are edible.

Dried
The dried leaves do not retain their color and flavor particularly well and are best used in cooked dishes.

CINNAMON

This wonderfully aromatic and versatile plant is widely used in the kitchen, in sweet and savory dishes. It also has medicinal applications, as does the oil extracted from this exotic tree.

The warming, exotic aroma of cinnamon conjures up all kinds of images—from cakes, breads, and cookies, and hot, milky drinks sprinkled with the rich brown powder, to spicy winter punches and meat dishes with a Middle Eastern or North African flavor. Mixed with other herbs and spices, such as bay and cloves, you can create all kinds of interesting culinary bouquets.

There are well over two hundred species of trees and shrubs within the *Cinnamomum* genus, found in eastern parts of Asia and Australia. *Cinnamomum zeylanicum* is the important spice cinnamon. It was considered a highly significant factor in the history of colonial power games. The Dutch largely controlled the worldwide cinnamon trade during the 1700s and early 1800s, and the spice is still very widely used and valued today. Closely related species are *Cinnamomum camphora*, from which camphor and camphorated oil are extracted, and *Cinnamomum cassia*, used for its bark, fruits, and oil.

Vital Ingredient

A substance called "cinnamaldehyde" is found in the bark and bark oil of *Cinnamomum zeylanicum*, which gives a distinctive flavoring and aroma to a wide variety of different products.

Oil can also be distilled from the leaves and is much more subtle than the pungent oil distilled from the tree's papery inner bark. In summer, small yellowy white flowers are borne, and the oval fruits that follow are purple in color.

Trunk
The bark on twigs and branches is papery in texture and light brown. The inner bark, either in stick or powdered form, adds a strong, sweet, and warm flavor to all kinds of foods.

USES

PARTS USED:
Inner bark, leaves, oil.

PROPERTIES:
Pungent, warming; stimulates circulation, lowers fever and blood pressure; controls bleeding and improves digestion.

USES OF THE HERB:
Culinary
Cinnamon spice adds a familiar, warm flavor to all kinds of foods—from cakes and breads to exotic meat dishes. The spice is used on a wide scale commercially, to flavor the same types of food, as well as sweets, soft drinks, ice cream, and pickles.

Medicinal
Use this stimulating herb during cold spells to boost circulation near the surface of the body, alleviate colds, and relieve arthritis and rheumatism. It revives the digestive system, helping with stomach upsets, soothes fevers, and controls bleeding and high blood pressure.

Cosmetic
Bark, bark oil, and the delicate leaf oil are used in cosmetics, perfume, and oral hygiene products.

CAUTION
Pregnant women should avoid cinnamon remedies.

CITRONELLA

An aromatic plant prized for its fragrant oil that has a wide range of applications—popular with aromatherapists, it is also used for its many healing properties.

The word "citronella" conjures up the grassy, lemon-rose fragrance of a citronella candle wafting across a patio or garden on a warm summer's night. The aromatic ingredient in these candles is citronella oil, extracted from the oil-rich tropical grass *Cymbopogon nardus*. This grass is widely grown for commercial oil extraction, from its native Sri Lanka and Java to South America and Africa.

Mosquito Repellent

Best known as a natural insect repellent, especially against mosquitoes, this oil was once often combined with Virginian red cedarwood oil in commercial products before the advent of chemical sprays. Today, citronella candles and sprays are still used as natural repellents or simply to fragrance a room. The fragrant oil is also used extensively as a base for many perfumes and particularly in less subtle products such as household soap. It is also added to other oils.

Effective Tonic

This stimulating, warming oil is also a favorite with aromatherapists. An effective general tonic and diuretic, it can be massaged into painful joints and stiff muscles to relieve discomfort, stimulates the digestive system, improves appetite and aids digestion, tones the kidneys, eases menstrual problems by stimulating blood flow, lowers fever, and helps expel intestinal worms. Psychologically, it clears the head, especially when combined with lemon essential oil. Citronella also has a similar scent—and similar properties—to lemon balm (*Melissa officinalis*).

As a personal hygiene and beauty aid, the oil's strong deodorizing and astringent effects make it helpful for excessive perspiration and for oily skin. Simply put a couple of drops on cotton wool and wipe gently over greasy areas (having first tested for sensitivity on your inner arm).

Leaf
Long, thin leaves have a fragrant lemony scent.

Stem
A rich source of citronella oil.

USES

PARTS USED:
Whole plant; oil.

PROPERTIES:
Diuretic, stimulant, general tonic, aids digestion, stimulates blood flow, lowers fever, helps to expel intestinal worms, tones the kidneys.

USES OF THE HERB:
Medicinal
A stimulating, warming, and clearing oil that acts as an uplifting general tonic, both physically and psychologically. Improves blood flow, stimulating digestive, respiratory, and menstrual systems, lowering fever, expelling intestinal parasites, and easing muscular and joint pain. Used by the Chinese for rheumatic pain.

Cosmetic
An effective deodorant in cases of excessive perspiration. Helps to clear greasy skin—try a few drops on a pad of cotton wool on very oily areas.

Household
The oil is a useful natural room fragrancer and insect repellent. Use in the form of candles and sprays.

**CAUTION
Should not be used during pregnancy.**

Oil
This stimulating aromatherapy oil can be combined with eucalyptus to increase the vitalizing effect or with lavender to dampen it down.

Stem
Square, green stem also
has covering of fine hairs.

Seeds
Blackish brown;
used medicinally.

Leaf
Very large, wrinkled leaves
covered in fine hairs. Used
dried or oil extracted.

Clear Eye
An infusion of the dried ripe seeds
softened in water can be used to clear grit
from the eyes and draw out splinters from
the skin.

CLARY SAGE

A popular plant in perennial borders, clary sage has
a long tradition as a medicinal herb. It has culinary
uses, and is also reputed to guard against ill health.

This attractive, aromatic, and useful plant—one of the many different
species belonging to the genus *Salvia*—is cultivated for its leaves,
flowers and seeds. Clary sage leaves have a wide range of uses. In the
kitchen, fresh leaves are delicious fried in butter, while individual florets
of the striking, long-lasting flower heads are also suitable for eating and
make an attractive garnish in salads. The leaves yield a valuable oil
used in aromatherapy and cosmetics, and as a perfume fixative.

Herb of Good Health
Clary sage also has a reputation as a symbol of general well-being. Its
botanical name comes from the Latin words *salvere*, "to be well," and
clarus, meaning "clear." It is sometimes known as "clear eye," referring
to an eye wash made from the seeds—the eye wash is made by
macerating the seeds in cold water until they are soft and swollen. This
maceration also draws out splinters, thorns, or other foreign bodies
from the skin. Another name for clary is "muscatel sage."

Health Promoting
Because of the herb's power to relax spasms and stimulate the uterus,
it long ago became known as a women's herb, relieving menstrual
problems and other female ailments, although it does have other uses.
It can also aid digestion and help control vomiting.

Cultivation
Clary sage is a native of Syria, Italy, southern France, and Switzerland.
This beautiful, fragrant, and fast-growing plant will thrive in many
situations but does not like heavy or moist soils. It has been popular
with gardeners for thousands of years—largely as a talisman against
ill health.

USES

PARTS USED:
Leaves, flowers, seeds, oil.

PROPERTIES:
**Bitter, astringent, and warming;
mucilaginous seeds.**

USES OF THE HERB:
Culinary
**Dip fresh young leaves in batter and
fry in butter. Try fresh individual florets from the flower heads in salads.**

Medicinal
**Controls vomiting, relaxes spasms,
stimulates the uterus and appetite,
calms nerves, and treats menstrual
problems; used as a soothing eye
wash to remove foreign bodies from
the eyes.**

Cosmetic
**Clary oil has a strong, ambergris-like
aroma; used in aromatherapy, it is a
powerful relaxant and induces a feel-
ing of euphoria; also used in soaps
and cosmetics, and as a fixative for
perfumes.**

Decorative
**Fresh or dried flower sprigs make
lovely arrangements.**

CAUTION
**Clary sage should not be taken in
large doses over a long period of
time. Pregnant women should avoid it.**

CLOVE

One of the most popular and versatile of all the spices, cloves are used in sweet and savory dishes and have a variety of medicinal applications.

The small, dark brown, club-shaped spice we know as a "clove," is actually the whole dried and unopened flower buds of a small evergreen tree. This tender native of Indonesia is today widely grown in warm, tropical regions.

Warm and Spicy
Cloves have an instantly recognizable aroma and flavor—exotic, warm, and spicy. They can be added to all kinds of dishes, from milky desserts and fruity dishes to savory sauces, marinades, and curries. Cloves are especially good with apples or studded into hams. They also make the perfect addition to winter drinks, and they are used for a range of preserves and pickles. Ground cloves give a traditional flavor to cookies and cakes.

Pain Relief
Clove oil, which is extracted from the buds, is also valuable—not just as a flavoring, but also as a strong painkiller. This highly effective antiseptic agent is a well-known way of temporarily easing toothache. It can also be applied to bites and will bring relief to rheumatism. Links with the mouth probably date back to the days of ancient China, where cloves were used to freshen the breath—the idea is simply to chew a single clove slowly. The Chinese also valued this warming, stimulating spice for its ability to improve digestion, calm nausea, and boost the functioning of the kidneys.

Centuries later, cloves were in use in Europe and were, for example, a common ingredient in Elizabethan pomanders. They are ideal for adding to potpourri, and the oil is used in various perfumed products.

Warmth and Sun
This tropical species needs sun, warmth, and well-drained, fertile soil. Flower buds are picked when fresh and pink in color, before they open. Oil is extracted and the buds are dried to form the familiar kitchen cloves.

Leaf
Glossy, leathery green leaves are lance-shaped, aromatic, and pink in color when young.

Flowers
Fragrant flower buds come in late summer and early autumn.

Dried Cloves
The flower buds are dried and used as a flavoring ingredient.

Clove Pomander
Make a traditional pomander, to place in a drawer or hang in a cupboard or wardrobe, by studding a fresh orange with cloves.

USES

PARTS USED:
Flower buds and oil.

PROPERTIES:
Warming, stimulating herb; antiseptic; controls vomiting and aids digestion.

USES OF THE HERB:
Culinary
Adds a warming, spicy note to curries, fruit dishes, marinades, cookies, and cakes.

Medicinal
A clove infusion can calm nausea and boost the digestive system, while clove oil massaged into the gums brings relief to toothache; diluted clove oil can be applied to ease rheumatism and to enliven tired feet.

Household
Use to add fragrance to homemade household soaps and for pomanders and potpourri.

Cosmetic
Used in perfume.

CAUTION
Causes uterine contractions, so is not recommended for pregnant women.

COCOA

This flavoring comes from the nutritious seeds of the cocoa tree. The paste extracted from the seeds is naturally bitter but becomes irresistible when sweetened with sugar.

Few can resist the fruits of the "chocolate tree." This tropical evergreen can reach well over twenty feet in height, and its small, pale flowers are unusual in that they spring directly from the branches. But *Theobroma cacao* is best known for its gastronomic qualities. The seeds—or beans—contained in its reddish-yellow fruit pods are fermented, dried, roasted, and then ground into a paste, the main ingredient of chocolate. Cocoa is naturally bitter in taste but is transformed by adding sugar. It is highly nutritious—hence the name "theobroma," which translates as "food of the gods." Chocolate is used in all kinds of desserts and baked goods, and chocolate flavoring is added to countless milky drinks and sauces.

Cocoa Butter

Cocoa beans yield an oil known as cocoa butter, widely used in cosmetics as a moisturizer and also by pharmacists to coat drugs and prepare suppositories. Both cocoa powder and cocoa butter have a variety of medicinal uses, based on their power to stimulate the muscles, kidneys, and heart. The alkaloid contained in the beans—theobromine—has a similar but milder effect to caffeine. It is a diuretic and can dilate blood vessels and so reduce high blood pressure. Externally, cocoa butter relieves chapped skin and burns.

Sweet Discovery

The Aztecs of ancient Mexico were the first serious cocoa drinkers, using it as the basis of a popular beverage called *chocólatl*. The explorer Columbus first introduced cocoa to Europe at the end of the 15th century, although it did not become popular until much later.

Variety of Flavors

The tree bears fruit that can be harvested year round but is cut mainly during early summer and late autumn. Different types of bean and processing methods produce a variety of chocolate flavors.

USES

PARTS USED:
Whole plant, leaves.

PROPERTIES:
A stimulating herb, both cooling and warming; contains volatile oils.

USES OF THE HERB:
Culinary
Cocoa beans form the basis of chocolate, used in many different ways. Chocolate flavoring is added to sauces, milky drinks, and some savory dishes.

Medicinal
Alkaloid theobromine in cocoa powder stimulates heart, kidneys, and muscles; diuretic and lowers high blood pressure by dilating blood
vessels; cocoa butter can soothe chapped skin and burns.

Cosmetic
Cocoa butter (also known as "oil of theobroma") is a very effective skin moisturizer.

CAUTION
Chocolate is a common trigger of allergies and migraines. Cocoa powder should be avoided by sufferers of irritable bowel syndrome.

Fruit
Fruits may be red, orange, or yellow, depending on variety; can be 6 in. long. Empty husks used as fuel, fertilizer, and animal food.

Confectionery
Plain or dark chocolate contains the most cocoa solids and the least sugar. Milk chocolate contains milk and sugar.

COMFREY

Comfrey has fallen out of favor as a culinary herb as it is thought that it may be toxic. However, it is still widely used medicinally and has practical uses in the garden as well.

Comfrey has long been used externally and is known for its impressive ability to heal wounds. Its properties are due to the presence of allantoin, a chemical that stimulates cell division.

Comfrey's botanical name, *Symphytum*, is also the name of a homeopathic remedy. It comes from the Greek for "unite" and thus recognizes its claimed ability to knit together broken bones. One of the old-fashioned country names for comfrey is "knitbone," and in the days before plaster casts, comfrey root was prepared and placed over an injury in a compress, where it would provide valuable support.

The flowering tops of comfrey contain vitamin B12, and the plant also contains calcium, potassium, and phosphorus. Traditionally, young leaves were eaten as vegetables, either raw or steamed like spinach. However, there are recent suspicions that it may be harmful if consumed in large quantities.

There are as many as twenty varieties worldwide. Some are cultivated as fodder—pigs are especially partial to it, and it is also given to racehorses.

In the Garden

Comfrey is a dense, hairy plant with purple, pink, or white flowers and is frequently grown by organic gardeners to energize the compost heap. Apart from its medicinal qualities, it is certainly decorative enough to include in any perennial border.

Choose its position carefully. Comfrey is deep-rooted and hard to move once established. But its long taproots can help to raise moisture and valuable minerals to the upper soil levels.

USES

PARTS USED:
Leaves and roots.

PROPERTIES:
Astringent, expectorant; soothes and heals and reduces inflammation.

USES OF THE HERB:
Medicinal
Apply comfrey root as a poultice over bruises, sores, or minor fractures that the doctor has decided not to set in plaster. Comfrey ointment is good for skin inflammation and other disorders including eczema. You can add an infusion of the leaves to bathwater. Comfrey is also used as a homeopathic remedy, Symphytum, for the same purposes.

CAUTION
Recent testing shows that comfrey contains alkaloids that, in very large doses, have been found to cause liver damage in animals. Although all comfrey preparations are considered perfectly safe for external use except on broken skin, while tests continue, it is advised that comfrey is not taken internally over long periods. Comfrey is subject to legal restrictions in some countries.

Leaf
Thick-ribbed and dark green. Contains more proteins than any other plant species; can be used to make a natural fertilizer.

Seeds
Small and very dark colored. Sow in autumn or spring.

Dried Root
Used in herbal medicine and to make tea.

Dried Comfrey
Comfrey tea has been used to cure stomach ulcers and throat ailments. However, it has recently been suggested that high dosages may be toxic.

CORIANDER

This aromatic herb has many culinary uses as well as healing properties. It is easily grown from seed—the fresh leaves and crushed seeds can be included in a variety of dishes.

Coriander leaves and seeds are a well-known flavoring in many Middle Eastern and Southeast Asian dishes—such as curries and chutneys. The plant also has many healing properties.

This strong-smelling herb has been cultivated for cooking and medicinal applications for at least three thousand years. It was first brought to Britain and northern Europe by the Romans, who used it as part of a mixture that was rubbed into meat to help preserve it. Coriander's preservative qualities were noted by the Chinese, who believed that it helped people live to a great age. It is, in fact, sometimes known as "Chinese parsley."

The plant was named "koriandron" by the ancient Greeks, who thought it smelled like bugs or *koris*. The smell of the leaves is very distinctive and not to everyone's taste. The seeds smell quite different from the plant, however, and can even be used in potpourri.

Healing Properties
Like its relatives caraway, dill, and fennel, coriander has healing properties related to the digestive system. It can be used instead of dill to make gripe water (a colic cure).

Coriander can act as an appetite stimulant and in this respect is sometimes used in the treatment of anorexia nervosa.

The plant itself has wispy foliage and a profusion of tiny pinkish-white flowers, and for this reason it is best planted in a drift.

Leaf
Mature, lower leaves look like parsley but have a strong scent. Upper leaves are wispy and have the same scent.

Stem
Fine, round stems can become straggly and branching. Can be chopped and used in soups and stews.

Seeds
Small, round, and light brown. Seeds can be collected by shaking the seed head after they gain full color. Strong-scented, the seeds are also ground and used in powder form. Flavor matures in storage.

USES

PARTS USED:
Leaves, seeds

PROPERTIES:
A strongly aromatic herb with preservative qualities and healing properties associated with the digestive system.

USES OF THE HERB:
Culinary
Coriander seeds are delicious with meat, especially pork. The leaves make a welcome addition to salads and can be included in curries and stews.

Medicinal
For an infusion, pour a cup of boiling water onto one teaspoon of crushed seeds and leave to infuse for five minutes. Drink before meals in order to relieve indigestion and flatulence. Coriander is useful to relieve period pain and was once used to help childbirth. If a breastfeeding mother drinks coriander tea, it will help relieve colic in the child, since its antispasmodic effects pass readily into breast milk.

Household
Use coriander seeds in spicy, warm-scented potpourri.

CRANBERRY

The tart berries of this hardy evergreen are used in sweet and savory dishes. High in vitamins A and C, they also make a useful home remedy for cystitis.

Tasty but tart, cranberries are delicious lightly cooked and eaten or used as a juice, or an ingredient in both sweet and savory dishes. There are two species used commercially and medicinally—the large North American *Vaccinium macrocarpon* and the small European *V. oxycoccus*. They have similar uses and properties, but most products come from the American species, which is more prolific. It is widely grown and produces shiny, juicy berries—cranberry sauce is a staple accompaniment for roast turkey eaten at Thanksgiving and Christmas.

Preserving Practice
As cranberries are rather sour, they are usually best preserved as jam or jelly (their high pectin content makes them particularly suitable for this), or combined with other fruit. They make delicious pies, sorbets, and ice creams, and may be eaten with fish such as rainbow trout or mackerel or added to gravy with roast duck, game, lamb, or chicken dishes. They should be cooked until the skins burst before adding sugar.

Cystitis Remedy
The juice is refreshing alone or with other fruit juice, and it is also a home remedy for cystitis. Rich in vitamins A and C, cranberries also contain a number of acids that make them highly antimicrobial and antiseptic, helping to prevent harmful bacteria accumulating in the bladder and urinary system. Cranberries are used to treat prostate problems and infections of the urinary tract. The berries also help to control asthma; simply skin, crush, and boil them in a little distilled water and drink, diluted with warm water—they have an active ingredient similar to that used in asthma drugs. Cranberries also improve circulation.

Thanksgiving Tradition
Native Americans combined the dried berries with meat to make a food called "pemmican," stored through the winter. The berries later came to the attention of settlers, who began to eat them with wild turkey— hence the Thanksgiving tradition.

USES

PARTS USED:
Berries, juice.

PROPERTIES:
Antiseptic, rich in vitamins A and C; helps to control asthma, stimulates circulation.

USES OF THE HERB:
Medicinal
Juice good for preventing and treating cystitis. Prescribed for prostate problems and asthma. Research indicates the presence of a polymer that can help to prevent infections of the bladder and urinary tract.

Culinary
Cooked fruit used in sweet and savory dishes, including pies, ice cream, sorbet, and meat gravy. Cranberry sauce traditionally eaten with roast turkey at Thanksgiving and Christmas. Juice makes a refreshing drink.

CAUTION
The berries are as acidic as lemons and should not be eaten raw in any quantity.

Sauce
Cranberries are the traditional accompaniment to roast turkey, whether in the form of a sauce or a glaze applied during roasting.

Fruit
Tart, ruby-red berries.

Leaf
Small, rounded, and bluish-green in color.

Stem
Delicate, creeping, and reddish in color.

DANDELION

This plant, with its bright yellow flowers, self-seeds and spreads readily to become a garden weed, but it is not all bad news—it has a variety of medicinal and culinary uses.

The common dandelion means different things to different people. Hated by many gardeners as a tenacious weed, this familiar, bittersweet plant, topped by distinctive yellow flowers, has a long history as a medicinal and culinary favorite. Dandelion's less-than-charming colloquial names include "swine's snout" and "piss-the-bed," due to its strong diuretic properties—it is used to help relieve a range of urinary problems. In India and elsewhere, dandelions are often used to treat liver complaints. Fresh leaves can be blanched and used in salads or cooked rather like spinach. The plant is also used in certain drinks.

Worldwide History

Dandelions have appeared in the botanical and medical literature of many diverse peoples—Middle Eastern, ancient Roman, Chinese, and European—since early times. For Elizabethan herbalist, John Gerard, the dandelion was part of the herbal medical canon. Its name is derived from the Arabic word *tarakhshaqún*, meaning "bitter herb," referring to its chicory-like flavor, making it a particularly popular vegetable in parts of France.

Family Connections

This perennial species belongs to the daisy family and, along with its many close relatives, is found across the world's more temperate regions, including South America. It is extremely hardy, surviving temperatures down to -20°F. Single, bright yellow blooms borne on leafless stems, and often deeply and unevenly serrated leaves, give the plant a highly distinctive appearance. During autumn, tiny seeds with fine, silky white hairs form a delicate sphere, or "clock," ready to be dispersed by the wind—and by generations of young children. New dandelion plants can be propagated by sowing seed in spring or by taking root-cuttings.

Leaf
Often with deep and uneven lobes, the nutrient-rich leaves form a rosette around the base of the stem.

Flower
Vivid yellow flowers have no center.

Stem
Purplish stems contain a milky sap, which is poisonous and an irritant, that can ease certain skin conditions.

Roots
Long, tough roots can be ground and used in caffeine-free coffee substitutes.

Dandelion Tea
Dandelion is well known for purifying the system. 1 tsp. of dried leaves, infused in about 1 cup of hot water, taken daily for a few weeks, is the recommended dose.

USES

PARTS USED:
Flowers, leaves, roots, whole plant.

PROPERTIES:
Bittersweet, cooling, diuretic, laxative; improves liver function and digestion; antirheumatic effects and reduces inflammation and swelling.

USES OF THE HERB:
Culinary
Fresh leaves can be added to salads, after being blanched to reduce their bitterness. Roots are also chopped into salads or roasted to make a coffee substitute.

Medicinal
Dandelion is recommended for some heart conditions, and as a diuretic—rich in potassium salts, dandelion replaces those lost due to taking a diuretic. Dandelion also boosts digestion and helps constipation, while its ability to reduce inflammation eases joint pain and skin problems.

Cosmetic
Fresh leaves added to a bath have a cleansing effect.

DILL

The ancients Greeks used it to cure hiccups, and since then it has been used to ward off evil and to make love potions. Today the leaves and seeds are used as a culinary ingredient—it's particularly suited as a flavoring ingredient with fish dishes.

An herb garden without dill is almost unthinkable. It is so versatile in cooking and so easy to grow that it is an ideal choice for any garden. Dill also has many medicinal benefits. Its name comes from the Saxon word *dilla* meaning "to lull," and the seeds have gentle tranquilizing properties.

The ancient Greeks found that dill cured hiccups, and the tradition of using it in preparations for infant colic has been passed down through the ages. Its uses have been recorded throughout history, from the Roman writer Pliny to the famous Elizabethan herbalist Nicholas Culpeper. Among more fanciful ideas, it was used to protect against witchcraft, and it has also been used for centuries as an ingredient of love potions.

Cultivation
The plant has wispy, feathery leaves, and in midsummer puts out tiny, highly aromatic yellow blooms arranged in clusters. Dill looks attractive when planted against a backdrop of marigolds and evening primrose and has the advantage of attracting insects that are beneficial to the garden.

Versatile Properties
Dill leaves contain magnesium, iron, calcium, and vitamin C, so it is beneficial to use them in salads, soups, and grilled meats. The seeds make an aromatic and pungent flavoring for pickles. Dill is particularly compatible with fish dishes—it is, for example, a main ingredient of the Scandinavian dish gravadlax and of dill mayonnaise for fish salads.

USES

PARTS USED:
Leaves, flowers, and seeds.

PROPERTIES:
Pungent, aromatic with cooling and diuretic effects.

USES OF THE HERB:
Decorative
Dill flowers look pretty when used as a filler in floral arrangements. There are different varieties, such as "bouquet" and "fernleaf," but they look similar.

Culinary
Use the seeds in soups, fish dishes, pickles, dill butter, and bread. You can add the flowering tops to a jar of homemade pickled gherkins, cucumbers, or cauliflowers. The leaves can be boiled with new potatoes and added to egg and salmon dishes. Dill is a main ingredient of the Scandinavian fish dish gravadlax.

Medicinal
Useful in a salt-free diet since it is rich in mineral salts. Dill water is good for indigestion, flatulence, and colic. Make by steeping a teaspoon of seeds in a cup of hot water, strain, and drink. Breastfeeding mothers can drink dill tea to pass the soothing properties on to their baby.

Cosmetic
Chewing dill seeds can help to clear up bad breath.

Leaf
Delicate, feathery, and blue green. Has an aromatic scent.

Stem
Normally only one stem per plant. Grows tall and branching in maturity, with umbrella-shaped flowers at top.

Seeds
Flat oval seeds can be gathered in summer and used to flavor savory dishes and puddings. Also infused to make dill water.

Dill Weed
Dried dill leaves are sold commercially as dill weed. The flavor is milder than leaves gathered fresh from a growing plant.

ELDER

This shrub or small tree has many attractive cultivars. It flowers in summer and produces berries in winter. It has many medicinal applications as well as some culinary uses.

The common elder—a deciduous shrub or small tree—has long been known for its many applications. The fragrant, creamy-white flowers and edible fruits are famous for the summer cordials made from them. Not only a delicious drink, the vitamin C-rich cordials are also recommended for tackling colds, coughs, and chest problems.

Medical herbalists prescribe elder remedies to lower fevers—drinking an infusion of elderflower water lowers the temperature by increasing perspiration. The healing and antiseptic leaves can relieve bruising or sprains, and they are also used as a natural, organic insecticide. Even the bark of these gnarled trees has been used to treat epilepsy, arthritis, and minor external burns, and the roots for kidney disorders.

The flowers of this versatile plant also appear in various cosmetic products and can be eaten—fried in batter to form fritters or used to add a fragrant, muscatel-like note to preserves, jellies, and fruit dishes. The tiny, dark fruits make a tasty sauce.

Country Wisdom
Commonly found across large areas of Europe, North Africa, and many parts of Asia, the elder has a centuries-old reputation as a traditional all-in-one natural medicine cabinet. It is also closely intertwined with gypsy folklore and the countless country superstitions of all kinds of peoples, and is mentioned in the works of William Shakespeare. The Russians believe that the elder will fend off evil spirits, while the Danes once thought that anyone standing under an elder tree would see the mythical king of the fairies go by.

In the Garden
As a garden shrub, the classic common elder is not favored as much as the more colorful cultivars that are available, but it is not unattractive. It will flourish in most gardens in either sun or partial shade, as long as the soil is kept moist and fairly fertile. It may be affected by blackfly in poor conditions.

Fruit
Clusters of dark berries, which are a good source of vitamin C but harmful if eaten raw.

Leaf
Pointed leaves grow in compound formations, with a row of leaflets either side of the midrib. When crushed, they release an unpleasant odor.

Dried Elderflower
Mainly used to treat colds, flu, catarrh, and sinusitis.

Elderflower Drink
A lovely summery cordial can be made from the attractive blooms that, according to lore, symbolize sympathy and compassion.

USES

PARTS USED:
Bark, flowers, fruit, leaves.

PROPERTIES:
Bitter, cooling, diuretic, pungent herb; lowers fever and reduces inflammation; anticatarrhal effects; antiseptic, healing, and insecticidal.

USES OF THE HERB:
Culinary
Flowers: in drinks, jams, and fruit dishes. Fruits: in cooked fruit dishes.

Medicinal
Flowers, fruits, bark, and leaves can be used for minor burns, wounds, **arthritis, rheumatism, and diarrhea; best known for lowering fever and to treat colds. Flowers used in skin preparations.**

Household
Leaves used in a natural insecticide.

CAUTION
Fruit and leaves are harmful if eaten raw.

EUCALYPTUS

The tonic, stimulating, and expectorant properties of the oil and leaves are exploited in all kinds of vapor treatments. It is also used as a flavoring in cough remedies.

The volatile oil and leaves of the eucalyptus gum or tree have such a wide range of applications that this must surely be one of the most useful additions to the herbal medicinal armory. There are over five hundred species providing an excellent source of timber—the timber was widely used in shipbuilding in the 1800s. It is also grown in various parts of the world, notably California, to dry out swampy ground. Today, the eucalyptus is mainly cultivated for its leaves, which yield volatile oils from small glands on the surface of the leaves. The various oils are highly valued and used for many different purposes. They were first produced commercially in 1860 in Australia, its country of origin.

Eucalyptus oil in general is both astringent and aromatic. Some species give an oil that is also mildly antiseptic and can tackle certain bacterial and fungal infections, making them highly useful for mouth and throat problems, wounds and sores, and conditions such as athlete's foot. The oil can also be effective as an anti-inflammatory, relieving conditions such as bruises, sprains and strains, muscular aches and pains, arthritis, neuralgia, and sciatica.

Distinctive Aroma
For many people, the smell of eucalyptus immediately conjures up cold cures. The stimulating, tonic, and expectorant properties of the oil and leaves are exploited in all kinds of vapor treatments, linctuses, inhalants, and rubs in clearing catarrh and easing bronchial and chest problems.

Around the Home
Outside the medicine cabinet, eucalyptus has a host of other uses. Its heady smell freshens the air quickly—so use dried leaves in potpourri or add a drop of oil—and its stain-removing powers mean that it is also included in various household products.

USES

PARTS USED:
Leaves; the bark is tapped for resin.

PROPERTIES:
Aromatic, astringent, stimulant, decongestant, and expectorant.

USES OF THE HERB:
Medicinal
Best known in treatments for coughs, colds, flu, chest and bronchial complaints, and excess catarrh. Some varieties are used to treat diarrhea, fever, wounds, herpes, muscular pains, and arthritis.

Household
The pungent leaves are perfect for potpourri and for use as an air freshener. Also used in detergents, insect repellents, and stain-removal products.

Cosmetic
Used in perfume, oral hygiene products, and skin creams.

Decorative
The fragrant leaves, often blue-green in color, are attractive in floral displays and wreaths.

CAUTION
The oil is toxic—use with care. Can cause skin irritation. Restricted in some countries.

Leaf
Aromatic and leathery, the leaves on young plants are often quite different in shape from those on mature trees.

Stem
Square and slightly winged, clasped by stalkless leaves.

Essential Oil
Eucalyptus oil is an antiseptic and is used to treat colds, respiratory problems and diarrhea; also acts as an insect repellent.

EVENING PRIMROSE

This herb, with its fragrant pretty flowers, makes an attractive garden ornamental. It also has many medicinal applications.

With its lovely primrose-yellow blooms opening at dusk and releasing a delicate scent, it is easy to see how this species earned its common name, although it is not related to the primrose. The species is also known as "tree primrose."

Evening primrose, and especially its seeds, is rich in fixed oil known as "essential fatty acids" (EFAs), that contains gamma-linoleic acid (GLA). The body manufactures GLA from essential fatty acids, which play a role in keeping hormonal, circulatory, nervous, and digestive systems functioning properly, thereby promoting all kinds of benefits, from healthy skin to correct bodily water levels.

Applications
The oil is used to ease symptoms associated with premenstrual syndrome (PMS) and menopause and has been indicated in a range of other conditions, from rheumatoid arthritis to cirrhosis of the liver.

Native American Healer
Originally from North America, the plant was introduced to Europe in the 1600s, via seeds in bags of soil used as ballast on cargo ships. Long ago, Native Americans ate the leaves and the nutritious, parsnip-tasting root as a vegetable and boiled the seeds to make a healing wound-dressing. By the 1900s, dried leaves and stem peelings were used as a treatment for ailments such as asthma, diarrhea, and water retention. However, the plant only became widely used in over-the-counter remedies when it came on to the scene in the 1980s, and it is now cultivated for its oil on a large scale—for medicinal capsules and in beauty and perfume products.

In the Garden
With its long-lasting supply of flowers, this plant makes a good garden choice—place it near outdoor seats to enjoy its scent. It produces a rosette of leaves in the first year and flowering stems the year after; sowing early may produce blooms the same year.

Seeds
Numerous tiny, pale-brown seeds yield valuable fixed oil consisting of essential fatty acids (EFAs).

Leaf
Lance-shaped leaves sometimes have slightly toothed margin. Leaves form rosette at base of stem, becoming smaller toward apex.

Stem
Erect, sturdy stem sometimes with fine down of hairs and red flecks.

Moisturizer
All kinds of cosmetic products now contain this healing, delicately scented oil, which is particularly effective for dry skin.

Healing Oil
Evening primrose oil is available in capsules and is widely used for premenstrual syndrome and menopause.

USES

PARTS USED:
Leaves, roots, and oil.

PROPERTIES:
Regulates hormonal system.

USES OF THE HERB:
Culinary
The chopped root can be used to garnish salads or eaten as a vegetable. Young leaves are also edible.

Medicinal
Especially good for promoting healthy, supple skin and eases conditions such as psoriasis and eczema. Also used in treatment of rheumatoid arthritis and coronary artery disease. Well known for relieving the symptoms of PMS and menopause, perhaps by helping to restore hormonal balance. May help with hyperactivity in children, cirrhosis of the liver, coughs, cystic fibrosis, and multiple sclerosis.

Cosmetic
Used in skin, perfume, and beauty products.

CAUTION
Not to be used by those suffering from severe depression or temporal lobe epilepsy, or during pregnancy.

FENNEL

The various forms of fennel have a range of culinary and medicinal uses—in fact, most parts of the plant, including the seeds, widely used as a flavoring, are edible.

Fennel is one of the most familiar kitchen herbs. A well-known digestive aid, its strongly aniseed flavor and aroma add a unique touch to all kinds of fish dishes, salads, sauces, soups, and breads. The species *Foeniculum vulgare* has several forms. Well known *Foeniculum vulgare* var. *dulce*, otherwise known as "Florence fennel," "sweet fennel," or "finocchio," is a native of Italy and the Mediterranean. With its distinctive bulbous base, it is cultivated all over the world and is especially popular in Italy, where it is often eaten raw as a snack, simply dipped in olive oil. *Foeniculum vulgare* "purpureum," known as bronze fennel, is an attractive shade of brown and is slightly hardier than the usual green-leaved kind.

Medicinal Qualities
Fennel seeds can relieve colic, flatulence, and an irritated bowel, and extracts are included in laxatives and babies' gripe water (a colic cure). The root is particularly useful for urinary disorders, and the plant also relieves sore throats and gum disease. This potent herb should not be used during pregnancy. With its feathery leaves and yellow flowers, fennel is also attractive enough to be cultivated purely as a garden ornamental and makes a fine focal point for a mixed or perennial border.

Herb of Vigor
Fennel spread throughout central and northern Europe at the instigation of Emperor Charlemagne (742–814). Said to bestow courage, strength, and longevity, it was eaten by Roman warriors and was one of nine herbs held sacred by the Anglo-Saxons as having the ability to ward off evil. In medieval times, the seeds were eaten during the Lent fast to ward off hunger. Fennel was also said to keep fleas away if left in kennels and stables.

USES

PARTS USED:
Leaves, stems, roots, seeds, and oil.

PROPERTIES:
Aromatic, diuretic; relieves digestive problems, relaxes spasms, reduces inflammation, and increases milk flow.

USES OF THE HERB:
Culinary
All parts used variously in fish and vegetable dishes, salads, curries, pies, breads, soups, and sauces. Also used to flavor salami.

Medicinal
Digestive aid, diuretic, boosts lactation (but not to be taken during pregnancy), relaxes spasms, anti-inflammatory. Seeds combat flatulence and stomach disturbances; root effective for urinary complaints. Use as mouthwash and eye bath, and rub for bronchial congestion.

Cosmetic
Infused crushed seeds make a cleansing face wash. Add a few drops of essential oil to skin lotions.

Household
Add to potpourri.

CAUTION
Not to be taken during pregnancy.

Leaf
Triangular, feathery, and bright green, or bronze in *F. vulgare* "purpureum."

Stem
Round, erect; hollows with age.

Seeds
Ribbed, aromatic, and gray-brown.

Florence Fennel
Florence fennel, also known as "sweet fennel" or "finocchio," is a staple of Italian cuisine. It has a large, bulbous base that tastes of aniseed and can be eaten raw or cooked.

FEVERFEW

Two thousand years ago this herb was prescribed for the treatment of headaches, and it is still used effectively for migraines to this day. It is of limited culinary use.

A strongly aromatic herb that originated in the Balkan region, feverfew has been grown for centuries as a medicinal and ornamental plant. Feverfew's popular name derives from its reputation for healing. English herbalists of four centuries ago described it as good for aches and pains in the head. In fact, feverfew was being prescribed for this by the ancient Greeks almost two thousand years ago. Modern science has proven that the ancient lore was right. In 1985, a study of the effectiveness of feverfew affirmed its place in modern health care—especially in treating migraines. It is particularly effective with the type of migraines that are eased by applying warmth to the head.

Feverfew (either in leaf or concentrated form) also has strong anti-inflammatory effects. This can make it useful in the treatment of painful arthritis. Because it reduces muscle spasm, it can also help in the case of painful periods. Feverfew has also been effective in conjunction with other herbs (such as black cohosh and golden seal) in the treatment of tinnitus.

Garden Plants
Feverfew is a pretty, daisy-like plant, with soft green serrated leaves and stems that are sprinkled with small white flowers throughout the summer and autumn. It can look particularly decorative sown along walls and between paving stones or grown in clumps against darker green foliage.

Leaf
Aromatic, divided leaves vary in color from yellowish to bright green. Attractive foliage makes it a useful border plant.

Stem
Fine, branching stems give bushy growth from which long flower stems grow in spring.

Feverfew Tablets
In some patients, feverfew has demonstrated a better ability to reduce or cure migraine than any synthesized drug.

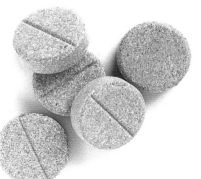

USES

PARTS USED:
Whole plant, leaves.

PROPERTIES:
Bitter, aromatic, pungent smell and nauseating taste.

USES OF THE HERB:
Culinary
Feverfew is very bitter, so its main uses are medicinal rather than culinary. But adding a few leaves to greasy foods will freshen them.

Medicinal
Eat one or two fresh leaves daily in a salad or sandwich, over a period of a couple of months, to help with migraine or period pain. Its effect is direct, but also preventative, so better results are seen over a period of time. Take also for hot flashes during menopause.

Decorative
Golden feverfew makes an attractive year-round plant for the garden. Use feverfew in pretty herbal wreaths and posies.

Household
Feverfew is an effective moth repellent. Place dried flowers and leaves in sachets. An infusion of the flower heads dabbed onto the skin will ease the pain of bites and keep other insects away.

CAUTION
Fresh feverfew can sometimes cause mouth ulcers. If this happens, try frying the leaf first. It is also a uterine stimulant and should be avoided in pregnancy. It should not be taken by people with a sensitivity to the daisy family. Lastly, it should not be taken by anyone on blood-thinning drugs since it affects clotting rates.

FOXGLOVE

Despite its toxicity, foxglove is a popular garden plant for its attractive, tall flowers. It is also commercially cultivated on a large scale to extract the heart drug digitalis.

The elegant foxglove, with its lovely blooms, makes an attractive garden plant but is highly toxic and should not be gathered for home use. Excess can cause side effects such as vomiting, visual disturbance, and loss of consciousness. The herb's potent properties come from the glycosides digitoxin, gitoxin, and gitaloxin.

Heart Drug
When grown commercially, its leaves are used to extract the widely used heart drug digitalis, which contracts the heart and arteries, raising blood pressure, and is used in cardiac medicine in cases of heart failure or irregular pulse. Homeopaths also prescribe it for kidney problems, migraines, depression, and insomnia.

Fairy Plant
The Anglo-Saxons called it *foxes glofa* (glove of the fox), and it was also known as "folksglove," referring to the "good folk," or fairies. The genus name *Digitalis* comes from the Latin word for finger, *digitus*, because of the way the bell-shaped blooms fit over the finger. The flowers' appearance is reflected in various other common names, including "bloody fingers." Its Norwegian name is *revbielde* (foxbell)—according to one legend, bad fairies gave the flowers to the fox, who used them on his toes to muffle his tread when out hunting.

The effect of digitalis on the heart has been recognized since early times—herbalists recommended foxglove for conditions such as epilepsy or delirium tremens, but today this kind of use would be considered dangerous. In North Wales, the plant had another use altogether—darkening the lines engraved on stone floors.

Precautions
Digitalis lanata—woolly foxglove—contains digitoxin, digoxin, and gitoxin, and is the main species grown commercially for medicinal use. Care should also be taken not to confuse toxic *D. purpurea* leaves with those of comfrey, which are similar in appearance. Despite their toxicity, foxgloves are popular in gardens, especially in traditional cottage gardens, for their tall, elegant flower spires—*D. purpurea* "Alba" has white flowers in summer.

USES

PARTS USED:
Leaves.

PROPERTIES:
Bitter herb that strengthens heart contractions.

USES OF THE HERB:
Medicinal
Leaves contain glycosides that strengthen heart contractions and raise blood pressure—used to treat heart failure and irregular pulse. Source of commonly used heart drug digitalis. Prescribed in homeopathy for kidney problems, depression, insomnia, and migraines. Formerly used for inflammatory diseases, delirium tremens, epilepsy, and other complaints.

CAUTION
Highly poisonous, not for home use—excess causes side-effects such as nausea, vomiting, loss of consciousness, and visual disturbances. Subject to legal restrictions in some countries.

Seeds
Of no medicinal use.

Flower
Bell-shaped, tubular, bright purple with mottled markings. Attracts bees and shelters smaller insects.

Leaf
Large leaves, dried and powdered for extraction of various heart drugs. Powdered leaf known as "digitalis."

Stem
Main stem with smaller, lateral shoots.

Leaf
Long, narrow, lance-shaped leaves.

Flower
Pale green, white-edged flowers bloom throughout the year in terminal spikes.

Rhizome
Orange-brown rhizomes contain a spicy, volatile oil.

Also known as Siamese ginger, galangal is used in a variety of spicy dishes in Southeast Asian cuisine.

GALANGAL

Originating from tropical rainforests, the growing regions of galangal are now more diverse. Similar to ginger in its culinary applications, galangal also has a range of medicinal uses.

Originating in the steaming forests of Southeast Asia, this plant has rhizomes with a distinctive ginger aroma—hence its other name of "Siamese ginger."

The rhizomes of this species—and the oil that they yield—are of culinary and medicinal value, although they are not as pungent as those of closely related *Alpinia officinarum*. *A. officinarum* is also known as "lesser galangal" and *A. galanga* as "greater galangal." In culinary matters, the rhizomes are enjoyed in much the same way as ginger, in a range of typical Southeast Asian dishes. The oil makes a good flavoring for various kinds of drinks.

Medicinally, this bitter herb is an effective stimulant for the digestive system—once again, much like ginger. In this role, it can help a variety of conditions, from indigestion to nausea and travel sickness. It may also help to reduce fever, although the more potent lesser galangal will usually prove more effective for this particular kind of problem.

In some parts of Asia, the volatile oil is included in certain perfumes.

Greater and Lesser
Both the greater and lesser *Alpinia* species have been used in the kitchen and in the pharmacy for many centuries, and were probably familiar to the Greeks. It was not until the 1800s, however, that the plants were officially given their genus name, when they were discovered in China and Southeast Asia by European botanists.

With their long, slender leaves and growing to a height of about five feet, galangal plants flower all year round, producing spikes of pale green flowers edged with white. These tender plants favor the warm, moist, and fertile conditions that mirror their tropical rainforest origins. Generally, their rhizomes are best lifted and used when they are about five years old.

USES

PARTS USED:
Rhizomes, oil.

PROPERTIES:
Aromatic and bitter; stimulates the digestive system.

USES OF THE HERB:
Medicinal
Much like ginger, the rhizomes of this plant can be used to settle the digestive system in many ways, relieving conditions such as nausea and travel sickness.

Culinary
Use the rhizomes fresh to give a mild gingery spice to stir-fries, curries, and all kinds of fish, poultry, and vegetable dishes.

GARLIC

This member of the onion family is known to have been regarded as a sacred herb by the ancient Egyptians. Apart from its culinary uses, it has also been recognized as especially benefitting the cardiovascular system.

Garlic is one of about seven hundred species of *Allium* or onion, long grown all over the world for their culinary and medicinal value. Garlic's distinctive, pungent aroma and flavor have made it one of the most popular culinary herbs. It is widely used in Oriental- and Mediterranean-style dishes. It is used raw in salads and dressing, and cooked in casseroles, stews, and roast joints of meat and poultry. It is also sometimes used with seafood.

Garlic is rich in strong-smelling sulfur compounds, which have a potent detoxifying effect on the body. It acts as an expectorant and, more important, has antibiotic and antifungal effects, and benefits the cardiovascular system. It is ideal for combating colds and other infections as well as helping to treat circulatory and bronchial disorders.

Asian Origins
The long story of garlic is thought to have begun in central Asia, and it was being cultivated in Mediterranean countries in ancient times. The Romans and the Greeks enjoyed garlic, while the Egyptians considered it to be a sacred herb—their slaves ate it to give them the strength to build the pyramids. Garlic appeared in English herbals from the 900s onward—the name comes from the Anglo-Saxon *gar* and *leac*, meaning "spear" and "leek," referring to the leaf shape. During the nineteenth century, much research was done to analyze garlic's healing properties, and certain active constituents were isolated. The herb was used as an antiseptic and to relieve dysentery during World War I.

Growing Your Own
Although native to warm climates, garlic can be grown in cooler regions. The outer cloves should be planted in fertile, well-drained soil, and new bulbs harvested after the leaves have died. Dry bulbs in the sun and store in a cool, but frost-free, place.

USES

PARTS USED:
Bulbs.

PROPERTIES:
Expectorant, cleansing, antibacterial, antifungal.

USES OF THE HERB:
Culinary
Garlic adds a classic touch to all kinds of foods—vegetables, meat, and fish—and is used widely in dips, sauces, and salad dressings, such as the traditional Mediterranean aïoli (garlic mayonnaise).

Medicinal
Used to relieve colds, flu, bronchitis, gastroenteritis, infectious diseases such as typhoid, and skin problems such as acne. Also an effective antifungal agent and a treatment for sore joints and rheumatism.

Cosmetic
A garlic hair rinse can ease dandruff. Apply in the evening and wash out the following morning to remove the smell.

CAUTION
Garlic can irritate sensitive skin.

Leaf
Narrow, flat leaves are gray-green in color and measure up to 2 ft. in length.

Garlic Cloves
The bulb of *A. sativum* consists of 5–18 bulblets or cloves. It is widely used for culinary purposes.

Stem
Long, delicate, and erect stems produce clusters of flowers in summer.

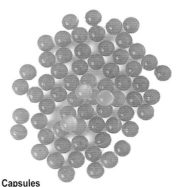

Capsules
For those who want to enjoy the benefits of garlic without any lingering smell, odorless tablets are widely available.

Bulb
The garlic bulb is encased in a papery, white or pink-flushed skin, with a clump of fine roots, similar to those of other onion species, at the bottom.

GARLIC CHIVES

Flowers
Flat, white, star-shaped flower heads with a sweet scent borne in late summer.

Subtle Flavor
Garlic chives, with a slight taste of garlic, can be used as a garnish or included in stir-fry dishes.

Leaf
Mid green, very long, narrow, and flattened; sheathed at base.

This member of the *Allium* family is less well known in the West than some of its other relatives, such as onions and garlic, but it is widely used in the East for its delicate flavor.

Garlic chives belong to the large and invaluable *Allium* genus, which also encompasses the familiar common onion (*A. cepa*), garlic (*A. sativum*), spring onion (*A. fistulosum*), and common garden chives (*A. schoenoprasum*). They are also known as "Chinese chives" or "cuchay" (the Chinese traditionally blanch garlic chives under clay pots or straw for eating raw, cut into finger-length pieces).

Mild Favorite
The mild garlic flavor of *Allium tuberosum* has made it popular in many parts of the world. Like all chives, it is best added to dishes toward the end of cooking, in order to preserve its taste. The long, slender leaves and flower buds of garlic chives are delicious added to Chinese stir-fried dishes, sprinkled fresh over omelets, salads and soups or mixed into cream cheese with a dash of lemon juice and seasoning.

Sulfur Compounds
Like all *Alliums*, chives contain sulfur compounds. These are responsible for the distinctive "oniony" aroma and also aid digestion, circulation, and respiration. Garlic chives are antiseptic and are prescribed for kidney and bladder problems, including urinary incontinence. The seeds (or *jui zi* in Chinese medicine) are taken for stomach chills accompanied by vomiting. Garlic chives may also be applied externally, combined with gardenia (*Gardenia augusta*) fruits as a poultice to soothe knee injuries.

Chinese Favorite
Chives have been a Chinese staple since the year 3000 BC and were sometimes used as an antidote for poisoning or to control bleeding. Although not as widely used as their close relative, the spring onion (*Allium fistulosum*), garlic chives were mentioned around AD 500 by Tao Hong Jin in his work *Ben Jing Ji Zhu*. They were introduced to European kitchens by the Venetian traveler Marco Polo in the 1300s and were also believed to ward off scab infection in animals.

Homegrown
Chives are easy and convenient to grow at home, ready for use in a container, but must be kept well watered. Like onions and garlic, they can help protect other plants from pests, weeds, and diseases.

USES

PARTS USED:
Leaves, flower buds, roots, and seeds.

PROPERTIES:
Improves kidney function.

USES OF THE HERB:
Medicinal
Taken for kidney and bladder problems, including urinary incontinence. Also for stomach chills with vomiting (seeds). Combined with gardenia

(*Gardenia augusta*) as a poultice for knee injuries in traditional Chinese medicine.

Culinary
Mild garlic flavor, easily destroyed by overcooking. Chop and sprinkle fresh over omelets, soups, salads, and baked potatoes. Blanch and add to stir-fries or pork dishes. Mix into cream cheese with a dash of lemon juice.

GARLIC MUSTARD

With its mild garlic flavor and the ability to grow where most other herbs will not survive, garlic mustard is a popular garden choice. It also has medicinal applications.

Flower
Small, pure white, and short-stalked followed by upright cylindrical pods.

Fruit
Narrow, upright pod around 2 in. long.

Stem
Erect, with fine hairs toward the base. Up to 4 ft. tall.

Leaf
Bright green; lower leaves heart-shaped with toothed edges; upper leaves more triangular.

Seeds
Tiny, dark brown seeds. Prompt sneezing when sniffed.

The erect stems and small, snow-white flowers of garlic mustard are often found in damp, shady spots. As its Latin and common names suggest, the chief characteristic of *Alliaria petiolata* is its pungent garlic aroma. The leaves can be picked when young and tender and added to salads and sauces—this is the origin of one of its traditional names, "sauce alone." Both leaves and stems contain the glycoside sinigrin, also found in several other members of the cabbage family, including the mustards *Brassica juncea* and *B. nigra*. This chemical possesses expectorant and anti-inflammatory properties, and can be prescribed internally as a treatment for bronchitis, asthma, and eczema. When the leaves and stems are applied in external poultice form, they can also relieve rheumatism, gout, and neuralgia, and can speed the healing of infected wounds and skin problems.

Country Flavor
Alliaria petiolata is also known as "hedge garlic," or "Jack-by-the-hedge" in the UK, and was a valuable addition to the rural diet, eaten with bread and butter and meat as well as in salads and sauces.

Infusions of the plant were once taken to induce therapeutic sweating or to combat worms, and its antiseptic qualities were used externally for gangrene and ulcers.

Fresh Juice and Leaves
Juice was extracted from the leaves and used alone or mixed with honey and boiled into a syrup for treating dropsy. When eaten fresh, the leaves were said to warm the stomach, boosting digestion. Cows were discouraged from eating the plant, however, as it imparts an unpleasant flavor to their milk.

Easy to Grow
Alliaria petiolata is the only member of this species worth planting in a garden, partly because it can survive in damp, dark places where other herbs would not grow well, if at all. It is easy to grow and self-seeds readily. Sow seeds in the spring directly into the soil.

USES

PARTS USED:
Leaves and stems.

PROPERTIES:
Pungent, stimulant, expectorant; anti-inflammatory effect and encourages healing.

USES OF THE HERB:
Culinary
Tender young leaves eaten in salads and sauces—give mild garlic flavor.

Medicinal
Take infusions for bronchitis, asthma, and eczema. Apply as a poultice for rheumatism, gout, and skin ailments, and to clear infection and speed healing of wounds. Formerly taken to induce sweating and for dropsy.

Bract
Yellow-green flowers
sometimes develop on
the red bract.

Roots
The underground rhizome, often called
the root, is the part of the plant that is
used. It is actually a rootlike stem, from
which plant shoots and roots grow.

Dried Ground Ginger
Ground ginger is a popular
flavoring and can also be
used in a range of medicinal
liquids and infusions.

Stem
Above the ground,
the stem is thick,
upright, and reed-like.

Stem
Under the ground, the stem
forms a bulbous, aromatic
rhizome—the most com-
monly used part of the plant.

GINGER

Ginger is a warming herb with a pungent aroma and flavor that enhances all kinds of foods—from confectionery and cakes to curries and stir-fries.

The Greek word for ginger—*zingiberis*—has given this perennial its name. The distinctive, branched rhizomes (commonly called "ginger root") have all kinds of uses, both fresh and dried, and oil can also be distilled from them and used in various ways.

This herb has just as wide a range of effects on the body—ginger has the ability to stimulate blood circulation; promote perspiration; relieve pain and cramps; calm muscle spasms, nausea, vomiting, and coughing; boost the digestive system; and relieve colds and flu. It has a proven track record in helping to control travel sickness. Ginger features prominently in Chinese medicine, as a cure for conditions associated with "cold," such as colds and bronchial congestion, and with digestive upsets linked with "spleen deficiency."

Fresh, Dried, and Ground
Taking a cup of ground or fresh ginger infusion is an excellent way to purify the system and combat indigestion, while chewing ginger rhizome can soothe a sore throat. Use sliced or grated fresh ginger in dishes such as curry and ground ginger in cakes and cookies.

Cultivation Tips
There are about one hundred species within the *Zingiber* genus, all of which have aromatic rhizomes. *Zingiber officinale*, the classic ginger, has long, pointed leaves and, rarely, fragrant yellow-green flowers streaked with purple. Ginger plants should be treated as an annual or biennial since a reasonable length of time is required to produce good rhizomes. Remove the older ones when new plant shoots appear. Ginger rhizomes may be unearthed partway through the growing cycle if specimens need to be nonfibrous.

USES

PARTS USED:
Rhizomes, oil.

PROPERTIES:
Pungent, aromatic; expectorant; controls nausea; aids digestion and liver function; relieves pain; stimulates circulation.

USES OF THE HERB:
Culinary
Dried ground ginger is used in cakes, cookies, and various sauces, and commercially in sweets, soft drinks, and condiments (the oil is also used as a flavoring), while the rhizomes appear in all kinds of meat and vegetable dishes, including curries, marinades, and chutneys. Pickled, ginger appears in Japanese cuisine, while green ginger (young rhizomes) are often preserved and candied.

Medicinal
Ginger's antispasmodic, warming, circulation-boosting, and pain-relieving properties make it ideal for a wide range of problems, including nausea and travel sickness, rheumatism, sprains, colds, and flu.

Cosmetic
Ginger oil is used in some perfumes.

CAUTION
Avoid in cases of high temperature, inflamed skin, or ulcers of the stomach or intestines.

GINKGO

This ancient tree, which predates the evolution of mammals, comes from China. It is now being researched in the West to treat a range of ailments.

Known alternatively as the "maidenhair tree," this rare species—the only member of its genus—grows wild in central parts of China, where its sacred status means that it is also specially cultivated. Both the leaves and seeds of this tree are used, and their value is principally medicinal. The seeds help to fight fungal and bacterial infections, as well as helping with a weak bladder, asthma, and phlegmy coughs.

The astringent leaves boost the circulatory system, regulating heart-beat, easing varicose veins, and dilating blood vessels, while relieving respiratory congestion by widening the bronchial tubes—the Chinese commonly use ginkgo preparations for lung complaints. It is the special flavonoids in the leaves that help with blood circulation.

Allergic Responses
There is also evidence to suggest that this bittersweet herb can help to control asthma and certain allergic reactions. It seems that this is the only plant whose leaves contain substances called "ginkgolides," which inhibit the action of platelets in the blood, and this in turn modifies allergic reactions.

The seeds of the ginkgo have been a staple of Chinese medical wisdom, and this is a tree that has truly ancient roots—modern specimens are almost exactly like fossilized ones that predate the first mammals. This tree first appeared in the West during the 1700s, after seeds were brought from China and Japan. It grows to an impressive height.

Reproductive Habits
The ginkgo produces flowers—tiny female flowers and long, catkin-like male flowers—between April and May. Male and female flowers grow on separate plants—and must be grown together in warm conditions in order for fertilization and fruiting to occur. The tree's fleshy seeds ripen to a yellow-orange color and have a slightly rancid aroma.

USES

PARTS USED:
Leaves and seeds.

PROPERTIES:
Astringent; seeds have antibacterial and antifungal effects; leaves stimulate circulation and control allergic responses.

USES OF THE HERB:
Medicinal
Ginkgo is especially effective when treating the elderly since it helps to improve the blood circulation. It relieves bronchial problems and coughs. It also helps prevent the slowing of brain functions that occurs with age. Effective against asthma and certain allergies.

CAUTION
Be careful with dosages of ginkgo remedies—too much can cause unpleasant side effects such as vomiting, headaches, diarrhea, and skin rashes.

Leaves
The leaves of this long-lasting tree turn a pale yellow during autumn.

Leaf
Leathery, fan-shaped leaves with a notched edge. Borne singly and often divided into two distinct lobes.

Stem
The stems have no medicinal use.

Radical Remedies
It is thought that ginkgo remedies may control the production of free radicals, which can harm the tissues of the body. They are also said to stimulate mental activity, especially in the elderly.

GOOD KING HENRY

The young shoots of this plant were once enjoyed in much the same way as we eat asparagus today. The flowers are edible, and the plant has some medicinal uses.

Once one of the most nutritious and widely used culinary herbs, Good King Henry is not so commonly used today. The plant's young, tender shoots are best picked when they reach around six inches in height and can be blanched like asparagus—they are quickly dipped in hot water and then rinsed in cold.

Flower
Minute greenish-yellow flowers borne in early summer.

Leaf
Triangular in shape.

Stem
Young shoots can be blanched and eaten like asparagus.

Culinary Uses
The flowering spikes are suitable for steaming. Both shoots and spikes are delicious served hot with melted butter or cold accompanied by a vinaigrette. The young leaves can be added to salads, while the larger leaves make an unusual and tasty spinach substitute in a wide range of hot savory dishes such as stuffing, casseroles, soups, and pies.

Gentle Laxative
Because of its high iron content, Good King Henry is particularly good for those with anemia, but extracts should be avoided by anyone suffering from a kidney complaint or rheumatism. The seeds have a mildly laxative effect and are especially useful for children with constipation, and an ointment or poultice of Good King Henry may help heal skin problems.

Good and Bad Henrys
The herb's name is under dispute: it was either named in honor of King Henry IV of Navarre, and was given the prefix "Good" to avoid confusion with the poisonous herb Bad Henry (*Mercurialis perennis*); or it was named after "Good Henry," an elfish character in Saxon lore.

Alternative Names
This herb also goes by a variety of alternative names, including "good neighbor," "wild spinach," and "Lincolnshire asparagus." Other members of the *Chenopodium* genus include the potent *C. ambrosioides* (wormseed) and *C. album* (fat hen), another popular pot herb.

Although rarely prescribed for human use today, this herb is still employed as a cough remedy for sheep. The seeds are also used commercially in the making of shagreen, a kind of artificial leather. The leaves and shoots of Good King Henry have been gathered for potting since Neolithic times.

USES

PARTS USED:
Seeds, tender shoots, and flowers.

PROPERTIES:
Nutritious, high iron content, gentle laxative, may help skin to heal.

USES OF THE HERB:
Medicinal
Apply externally to skin sores. Seeds mildly laxative, especially suitable for children. Cough remedy for sheep.

Culinary
Blanch young shoots like asparagus and serve warm with butter or cold with vinaigrette. Steam flower spikes and eat leaves raw in salads or use as spinach substitute in soups, pies, stuffings, and casseroles. Highly nutritious.

HAWTHORN

Smell the flower of the haw and it can only be spring—according to folklore, a time for rejuvenation and fertility rites to make the pulse race and the heart healthy.

Flower
White flowers bloom in May.

The hawthorn is one of the most familiar plants of traditional European folklore—the fragrant white spring blossom of this small tree or shrub is a well-known symbol of fertility. The name *Crataegus* comes from Greek words meaning "hard," "sharp," and "thorn." The species *laevigata* and *monogyna* are almost identical, except that monogyna leaves are more deeply lobed and the fruit contains only one seed. Both species produce bloodred berries with the same medicinal properties, mainly used to improve the circulation and aid hypertension and heart problems. (Note: patients with heart conditions should not take herbal remedies without consulting a qualified practitioner.) The berries are antibacterial, diuretic, and astringent, stimulating the digestive system and uterus, and are used in Chinese medicine to treat irritable bowel syndrome, absence of menstruation, and postnatal pain.

Symbol of Life and Death

In pagan times, hawthorn was the center of fertility rites, including the custom of going "a-Maying" and crowning the May king and queen. But, as the king and queen were sacrificed in the belief that this would ensure a good harvest, the plant also has connotations of doom and death—many still think it unlucky to bring hawthorn into the house. Christ's crown of thorns was thought to have been hawthorn, while the flowers were said to hold the lingering odor of the dreaded black plague that struck during the fourteenth century.

Young hawthorn leaves may be added to sandwiches and eaten—hence the country names "ladies' meat" or "bread-and-cheese"—and the fine timber was used as fuel and to make boxes and combs. Hawthorn has always been popular as hedging—*haw* is an Old English word for hedge.

Leaf
Oval leaves more deeply lobed in *C. monogyna* than in *C. laevigata*.

USES

PARTS USED:
Fruits.

PROPERTIES:
Warming herb; improves peripheral circulation; regulates heart rate, blood pressure, and coronary blood flow.

USES OF THE HERB:
Medicinal
Stimulates circulation, digestion, and uterus. Used as a heart tonic since the Middle Ages—good for angina, irregular heartbeat, high blood pressure. Used in Chinese medicine to combat irritable bowel syndrome, absence of menstruation, and postnatal pain. Berries and flowers used for circulatory conditions, and juice as digestive aid. Antibacterial and diuretic; once taken for dropsy.

CAUTION
Anyone with a heart condition should consult a qualified practitioner before taking hawthorn remedies

Fruit
Small, bloodred berries; used as a heart remedy since the Middle Ages.

HEDGE MUSTARD

Salad Dish
Add young leaves to salads for an unusual mustardy flavor.

Flower
Tiny yellow blooms.

Stem
Like the leaves, the round stem is also silvery and woolly, turning woody and brownish toward its base.

Leaf
Hairy leaves with distinct lobes.

The ancient Greeks prescribed hedge mustard mixed with honey as an antidote to poisons and inflammation. It is still prescribed medicinally, and the young leaves have some culinary uses.

This common weed—a hardy annual—is often found liberally covered with dust, growing along roadsides and on waste ground across much of the world—North and South America, Europe, Africa, and western parts of Asia.

Peppery Plant

With constituents that include glucosinolates and a glycoside, the common hedge mustard, *Sisymbrium officinale*, bears some similarities to mustard plants and has a peppery aroma. It also contains a compound that affects the heart. All parts of the plant, including the flowering heads, can be used in medicinal preparations and infusions. Its expectorant properties make it ideally suited to clearing a variety of bronchial, throat, and catarrhal conditions. Used as a culinary plant, the young and tender fresh leaves add a piquant flavor to leafy salads, sauces, and soups.

Voice Restorer

Ancient Greek physician Dioscorides, author of *De Materia Medica*, the highly influential Western herbal work, recommended mustard plant preparations to counter infection or poisoning. Infusions were also traditionally taken for a whole range of throat problems. In France, up until the mid-1700s, the plant was especially well known for its ability to restore a lost voice—hence another common name, "singer's plant."

Propagation

This annual—one of eighty species in the genus—will sometimes last through the winter and can be propagated by sowing seeds in either spring or autumn. Sow seeds in acid to alkaline, moist to dry, soil. It tolerates partial shade.

The branched stems have long terminal spikes of unremarkable pale-yellow flowers, which bloom through the later part of the summer—the flowering tops can be used for making infusions. The main stems are slim but very tough, with a rosette of compound leaves at their bases. The leaves can be picked in spring and used fresh.

USES

PARTS USED:
Leaves, flowering tops, whole plant.

PROPERTIES:
Tonic, laxative, diuretic, and expectorant; aids digestion.

USES OF THE HERB:
Culinary
Add tender young leaves to salads, sauces, soups, and egg dishes such as omelets.

Medicinal
Taken internally, this expectorant helps to clear conditions such as bronchial congestion, catarrh, coughs, and laryngitis. Improves digestion and acts as a diuretic and laxative.

CAUTION
Large doses can affect the heart.

HEMLOCK

This deadly narcotic herb has been used for thousands of years for its medicinal effects and as a sedative. It was also used by the ancient Greeks to execute convicted criminals.

Famed as a highly toxic poison since the time of the ancients, this bitter wayside herb bears a dangerously close resemblance to other harmless, parsley-like plants. Hemlock is, in fact, also known as "poison parsley." Several parsley-like herbs self-seed very easily, so any parsley cultivated for culinary use should always be grown in an easily identified spot, well away from similar-looking species that may be toxic.

Temperate Species
Naturalized in North and South America, *Conium maculatum* is also found in Europe, western Africa, Asia, and Australia, preferring temperate regions. Despite its dangers, this sedative, anesthetic herb has a history of medicinal use—but it must only be prescribed by qualified practitioners. The whole plant is highly toxic and should never, under any circumstances, be used at home. A hemlock remedy is prescribed by homeopaths for several conditions, including depression and dizziness. The herb is also used externally by medical practitioners for certain types of tumor, hemorrhoids, and mastitis.

Poison Symptoms
Excess hemlock causes suffocation by paralyzing the respiratory system, due to certain alkaloids (mainly coniine) present in the plant, and death can follow. Symptoms of hemlock poisoning include difficulty with breathing, dilated pupils, torpor, and paralysis.

Herb of Ancient Greece
Hemlock was being used medicinally in Ancient Greece, and the genus name *Conium* actually comes from the Greek word for hemlock, *koneion*. The ancient Greeks used the herb for a range of ailments, from epilepsy to asthma. The Greeks also employed hemlock to execute convicted criminals—Socrates, the great Athenian philosopher, was condemned to death for his bold ways of thinking and met his end by drinking hemlock in prison, surrounded by a group of his followers. Over the years, mistaking the leaves for parsley has caused many poisonings, as has the use of the hollow stems as whistles by children. The plant is best avoided, as is anything resembling it that cannot be identified with certainty.

Flower
Umbels of small white flowers resemble several nonpoisonous species; blooms from July to September.

Leaf
Feathery, parsley-like leaves, broadly oval in shape and much divided.

Stalk
Characteristically spotted dark purple.

USES

PARTS USED:
Leaves and fruits.

PROPERTIES:
Narcotic; sedates and relieves pain.

USES OF THE HERB:
Medicinal
For use by qualified practitioners only. Prescribed for depression and anxiety, certain glandular and eye problems, thickened arteries, and dizziness; added to ointments or oils and applied externally for tumors, mastitis, and hemorrhoids.

CAUTION
Beware—whole plant can be fatally poisonous if eaten and is a skin allergen; for use by qualified practitioners only. Legally restricted for medicinal use in some countries.

HOREHOUND

Flower
Whorls of small, creamy-white blooms appear in summer.

Leaf
Gray-green and felty with deep wrinkles and toothed edges. Arranged in pairs.

Stem
Hairy and angular.

Known to the ancient Egyptians, horehound has a long history as a medicinal plant—it has been used to treat dog bites and expel worms and is now prescribed for coughs.

Horehound is a hairy, aromatic plant native to the Mediterranean and central Asia. It is also well established in fields and wasteland in other parts of Europe, North Africa, and the Canary Islands.

Medicinal Marrubiin

Horehound's medicinal powers spring from a potent expectorant, marrubiin, found in the whole plant, making it effective against asthma, bronchitis, catarrh, chesty coughs and colds as well as whooping cough. Today, it is often prescribed as a candied cough sweet but may also be used fresh or dried in cough syrups, infusions, various extracts, and powders. Antiseptic, antispasmodic, and anti-inflammatory, this species also stimulates perspiration and bile production, and acts as a sedative on the heart. It is used in small amounts to stabilize an irregular heartbeat, and also taken internally for liver and gallbladder disorders and typhoid fever. Applied externally, it can combat minor wounds and skin eruptions. Horehound is frequently combined with a number of other herbs, including *Zingiber officinale* (ginger) or *Thymus serpyllum* (wild thyme) for whooping cough and *Lobelia inflata* (Indian tobacco) for bronchitis. It is sometimes adulterated with oil from *Ballota nigra* (black horehound).

Egyptian Cough Remedy

The name horehound comes from the Old English *har hune*—"a downy plant." *Marrubium* probably originates in the Hebrew *marrob*, or "bitter juice"—it is said to be one of the five bitter herbs eaten by Jews at Passover to mark the exodus from Egypt. The plant has been used medicinally since Ancient Egyptian times and later became a household remedy for dog bites and worms. Horehound is also used by medical herbalists as a substitute for quinine in preventing malaria.

USES

PARTS USED:
Whole plant.

PROPERTIES:
Aromatic, antiseptic, expectorant; anti-inflammatory, antispasmodic, sedative effect on the heart; increases bile flow and perspiration.

USES OF THE HERB:
Medicinal
Contains marrubiin, a strong expectorant. Stimulates sweating and bile production and stabilizes irregular heartbeat. Taken internally for asthma, bronchitis, chesty coughs and colds, catarrh, whooping cough, liver disorders, gallbladder disorders, typhoid fever. Applied externally for small cuts and bruises and skin eruptions. Frequently combined with other herbs. Former antimalarial substitute for quinine.

Household
Once sprayed onto cankerworm in trees.

CAUTION
Should not be taken during pregnancy. Excessive use during lactation should be avoided. May affect menstrual cycle. Handling plants may cause dermatitis.

HORSE CHESTNUT

This large tree, often seen in city plantings, should not be confused with the sweet chestnut which has many culinary applications—the horse chestnut is mainly for medicinal use.

Although horse chestnut seeds look similar to those of the sweet chestnut (*Castanea sativa*), the two trees are unrelated. While sweet chestnuts are delicious in a host of dishes, horse chestnut fruits are fit only for animal fodder, and can be harmful to humans. However, both these nuts and the tree bark do have medicinal properties, contained in the powerful anti-inflammatory compound aescin, which is used in pharmaceutical preparations and is processed commercially to aid absorption into the body.

Applications
Horse chestnut is particularly effective in stimulating the circulation and tackling disorders such as hardening of the arteries, stroke, heart attack, chilblains, phlebitis, hemorrhoids, and varicose veins. Bitter, astringent, and diuretic, horse chestnut also helps to lower fever, relieve local edema, and reduce swelling. It is sometimes injected directly into swollen joints and fractures. Horse chestnut extracts also appear in some shampoos for dark hair, or in bath oils to help improve the skin.

Buckeye
Shiny and reddish-brown in color, the nuts gave rise to one of the tree's traditional names, "buckeye," reflecting their resemblance to the eyes of deer. *Aesculus* comes from the Latin *esca*, meaning food, while *hippocastanum* is a literal translation of the common name, "horse chestnut." The link to horses is unclear but does not seem related to the horseshoe-shaped leaf scars that cover the twigs. It may spring from the use of the nuts as fodder and a cough remedy for horses. During World War I, English trials showed that for every ton of horse chestnuts harvested as fodder, half a ton of grain was saved for human consumption. The horse chestnut was introduced to the West in the sixteenth century and has since become a common ornamental, often planted on streets and in parks.

USES

PARTS USED:
Bark and seeds.

PROPERTIES:
Bitter, astringent, diuretic, and anti-inflammatory; lowers fever and relieves local edema.

USES OF THE HERB:
Medicinal
Bark and seeds contain anti-inflammatory substance aescin, a combination of saponins. Aids circulation. Used for heart attack, hardened arteries, stroke, varicose veins, hemorrhoids, phlebitis, chilblains, swelling.

Cosmetic
Used in shampoos for dark hair and in bath oils.

CAUTION
Harmful if eaten. Do not treat serious circulatory disorders yourself.

Leaf
Large, palmate, divided into 5 or 7 leaflets, springing from a central point. Margins finely toothed.

Branch
Smooth, gray-green bark yields a yellow dye. Wood soft and spongy—formerly used for packing cases. Twigs covered in tiny, horseshoe-shaped leaf scars.

Fruit
Round, green husk, covered in short spines. Splits on falling to the ground to free the nut.

Seeds
Tiny brown, tear-shaped seeds.

Flower
The classic color of these nectar-rich flowers is purple-blue, but there are also pink and white forms.

Leaf
Narrow, lance-shaped leaves have a sage-like flavor and aroma.

Stem
Square-shaped stem; woody at the base.

Dried Leaves
A handful of crushed hyssop leaves, infused in boiling water and left to cool, is effective for treating bruises.

HYSSOP

Hyssop dates back to the Old Testament and the ancient Greeks who used it to purify the system. The leaves and flowers have culinary uses as well as medicinal applications.

Mention of this herb was made by the ancient Greek physician Hippocrates, often called the founding father of modern medicine. The name "hyssop" probably comes from a Hebrew word meaning "holy herb" and refers to its supposed purifying ability, reference to which is made in the Bible. With attractive flower spikes and a pleasant, sage-like smell, this compact, semi-evergreen perennial is always a good choice in the garden, as a low hedge variety, an edging plant, or an addition to containers. Both the flowers and the leaves are fragrant and can be used in various ways. The narrow leaves are pleasant—and aid digestion—when added to rich, meaty stews, casseroles, and soups, although their strong flavor means that they should be used in moderation. Flowers can be tossed into salads. Around the house, the plant's powerful aroma can be put to good use in potpourri—and as an effective insect repellent.

Medical Matters
As a medicinal herb, hyssop has a range of applications, but the essential oil must be used with care, in moderation—an excess can be potentially fatal. Employed wisely, however, the hyssop plants and their essential oil can tackle certain problems very effectively. External poultices help with chest problems, bruising, and cuts. Drinking an infusion of the flowering plant or flowers eases chest and respiratory problems, coughs, sore throats, fever, indigestion, and rheumatism.

Care of Hyssop
To promote healthy compact hyssop plants, especially in hedges, cut them back hard during the spring, trim after flowering, and replace totally after about five years.

USES

PARTS USED:
Whole plant, leaves, flowers, and oil.

PROPERTIES:
Aromatic, astringent, bitter, expectorant; anti-inflammatory and reduces fever; tonic effects.

USES OF THE HERB:
Medicinal
Drinking an infusion of this expectorant herb—two teaspoons in hot water, twice a day—will ease chest problems, coughs, and catarrh as well as indigestion. Externally, hyssop helps cuts, bruises, and rheumatism.

Culinary
Add sparingly to rich meat and fish recipes, as well as vegetable and pulse dishes.
Household
Effective in potpourri and as an insect repellent.

Decorative
An attractive addition to any herb garden.

CAUTION
Must not be taken during pregnancy. Excess hyssop essential oil can prove fatal or cause epileptic fits. The oil is legally restricted in some countries.

INDIAN LICORICE

The seeds of this plant are as pretty as the flowers they follow and are also extremely poisonous. Once a measure of weight in India, the seeds are now mainly used in medicinal applications.

Seeds
In India's thriving gem trade, the seeds have traditionally been used since ancient times to weigh precious stones and metals. One seed is taken to be one carat.

The distinctive scarlet and black seeds of this tender vine—a native of India's tropical forests and much of the tropics—are highly toxic if eaten, and their use is legally restricted in some countries. Eating just one seed can cause death. The roots of this species, which should also not be eaten, are very sweet—much sweeter than sugar—and its leaves have a licorice-like flavor, hence the common name.

Supervised Use
It is the leaves and seeds of *Abrus precatorius* that are traditionally used, and any part of this plant should only be used under qualified supervision. The licorice-flavored leaves can be taken to soothe coughs and sore throats, while poultices made from a seed paste can ease various skin problems, hair loss, and nervous disorders, including nerve pain. They have been used externally on conditions such as paralysis and leprosy, and were once applied to eye infections as they irritate the eyes and can help to "bring out" certain problems. This is not now recommended.

Leaf
Compound leaves are used in various preparations.

Unit of Measurement
In their native homelands, the seeds have a range of other applications too. They are worn widely as beads, and as a charm to ward off bad health, and are also used as prayer beads. Another name is *jequirity*, from Native American, meaning "lucky bean." The beads also make attractive ornaments. Since earliest times, the seeds have been employed as a traditional unit of measurement in India to weigh gold and gemstones. Used in this way, the seeds are known as *rati*. Indian history is also full of terrible tales of poisonings—both deliberate and accidental—at the hand of the seeds, and of children playing with these brightly colored objects and then eating them, with tragic results.

This is a plant that likes tropical conditions and needs good high temperatures to produce its blooms. It can be cultivated as an ornamental, given the right conditions.

USES

PARTS USED:
Leaves, seeds.

PROPERTIES:
A soothing, emetic, and irritant herb.

USES OF THE HERB:
Medicinal
Leaf infusions aid coughs and sore throats, while infusions and pastes made from the seeds have been used externally for skin and hair problems, as well as some nervous disorders.

Decorative
Seeds used as decorations and as beads but must be used with care and not eaten or chewed accidentally.

CAUTION
Seeds are extremely poisonous, and roots can also be toxic. Do not use unless under qualified supervision.

Fruit
The seeds are encased by pods (like miniature peapods), which appear after the flowers.

IVY

Commonly used as ground cover or as a climbing plant, ivy is also used medicinally to treat a range of conditions, including gout and rheumatic pain; externally it is used for cellulite, warts, and painful joints.

Glycerined Ivy
Preserving ivy with glycerine keeps the stems flexible and retains a shine on the leaves, making it perfect for long-lasting dried flower arrangements.

Flower
Yellow-green flowers bloom during the later months of the year.

Leaf
Dark green, with a distinctive angular shape, more pronounced in young foliage.

Ivy is a reliable, adaptable favorite with a host of gardening uses. Happy and easy to maintain as an indoor plant, it also thrives outside, forming quick-growing ground or trellis cover, or trailing attractively from a variety of pots and containers, coexisting readily with a range of other plants and flowers. Types with variegated leaves will need more light to keep their coloring and also tend to be less hardy. In ancient Greece, ivy wreaths were a feature of weddings, as the plant is also a symbol of fidelity.

Ringing the Changes

There are up to eleven species within the *Hedera* genus, some climbing and others creeping in habit. The stems are covered with adventitious roots—roots growing directly from the stem—that help the plant to cling as it spreads across a surface. The flowers of the ivy—yellow-green and rich in nectar—only bloom in sunny conditions, late in the season. The fruits are black and highly poisonous. There are over three hundred varieties of *Hedera helix*. Popular choices include *H. helix* "Erecta," an upright, bushy plant with small leaves; *H. helix* "Glacier," whose silver-gray leaves are edged with white; and *H. helix* "Goldheart," a good climber for sunny walls, with dark leaves that have a vivid yellow center.

Therapeutic Value

Taking ivy remedies must be supervised by a qualified practitioner, as the plant is highly toxic if eaten. It appears in a variety of forms, from poultices for joint and tissue problems to creams for skin eruptions and tinctures suitable for easing bronchial congestion.

USES

PARTS USED:
Leaves

PROPERTIES:
Bitter, aromatic; antibacterial and expectorant.

USES OF THE HERB:
Medicinal
Ivy is toxic, and preparations must only be taken under supervision. The plant has strong antibacterial properties and an ability to tackle fevers and spasms, and acts as an expectorant. Whooping cough, bronchial problems, rheumatism, swollen tissues, burns, skin eruptions, and toothache are just some of the diverse conditions that ivy preparations can help.

Decorative
Ivy, especially variegated types, always makes an attractive, robust addition to floral arrangements.

Cosmetic
Creams and lotions containing ivy are effective against sunburn and cellulite (by getting rid of toxins and excess fluid).

CAUTION
Every part of this foul-tasting plant is toxic and can cause skin irritation or allergic reaction. Use only recognized preparations from qualified herbalists.

JOJOBA

The natives of North America have long used the oil from jojoba to soften leather and for cosmetic purposes. Nowadays, it is used in many skin care products for its cooling, moisturizing properties.

Oil from the seeds of this evergreen shrub—a native of northwestern Mexico and the southwestern United States—has legendary skin-softening properties and is now used widely in the cosmetics industry.

Jojoba—pronounced "hohoba"—is cooling and soothing as well as unusually moisturizing, so it is used for a range of skin conditions, including sunburn and the much more problematic psoriasis. Apart from its cosmetic use, the oil also has more heavy-duty applications—as an engine lubricant and in certain detergents, for example. As it suits arid conditions, jojoba has also been used as a way of halting the land erosion that leads to desertification.

Native Americans

The name "jojoba" comes from Mexico. For many years, the Native Americans used the rich oil from the jojoba plant to soften their skin and hair. They also used it to process leather.

Plantations started to spring up in the late 1970s, and jojoba came to rapid prominence in the 1980s. This was largely due to bans on whaling and whale products—jojoba oil closely resembles sperm whale oil and so became a valuable, eco-friendly substitute.

Cultivation

The jojoba shrub is slow growing, and quality is all important. Mass production of top-quality plants has been advanced by tissue-culture methods of producing female plants (jojoba shrubs have separate male and female shrubs). Each female can produce a massive amount of seeds—up to ten pounds a year.

Jojoba is the only species in the *Simmondsia* genus. Its distinctive, leathery leaves are oval in shape, and females and males produce small flowers during the spring months—the male flowers are green and the female ones yellow. Jojobas are half-hardy and tolerate dry heat extremely well. They can be propagated either by sowing seeds or by taking different kinds of cuttings in spring and autumn.

USES

PARTS USED:
Oil extracted from the seeds.

PROPERTIES:
Soothing and softening.

USES OF THE HERB:
Medicinal
Jojoba's cooling, softening action is effective in helping skin conditions such as sunburn, acne, psoriasis, and flaking scalp.

Cosmetic
An important ingredient for a whole range of cosmetic, hair, and skin care products.

Household
Used in various detergents and lubricants.

Seeds
Also called nuts or beans, the ripe seeds produce richly moisturizing oil.

Leaf
Leathery, oval leaves are around 2 in. long.

Jojoba oil
Jojoba is a remarkable moisturizer and is used in a wide range of products to combat dry skin and hair.

Berries
Resinous, and found only on the female plant. Take up to three years to ripen, changing from green to dark purple or black when ripe.

Leaf
Silvery-green spiny needles appear in whorls of three, making the plant very prickly.

JUNIPER

Once widely used for its medicinal qualities, juniper has become more of a culinary flavoring—it is commercially cultivated and used to flavor game dishes and pâtés.

This bushy evergreen tree is cultivated for its berrylike cones, which give a distinctive flavor as well as possessing medicinal properties.

Juniper berries are widely used as a flavoring, especially in game dishes and pâtés. Oil is extracted from juniper to use in spicy fragrances. Nowadays, most commercial supplies are grown in southern Europe.

Juniper is slow growing, with silvery-green spiny needles and small yellow flowers in summer. The oily, resinous berries only occur on the female plants and take up to three years to ripen. One bush can possess several generations of berries at different stages of ripeness. Special bush varieties, from six to ten feet high, are also grown as ornamental garden plants. Both male and female plants must be grown together to produce berries on the females.

Healing Properties
Various juniper species are used medicinally, although some are too strong for internal use. Juniper has long been credited with cleansing properties. It can remove acid waste from the system and was once believed to cure many illnesses of the digestive system, gout, and kidney inflammation. It is an irritant and should not be taken by pregnant women. A powerful external cleanser, juniper can help with eczema, psoriasis, and even cellulite.

USES

PARTS USED:
Berries.

PROPERTIES:
An aromatic herb; antiseptic and diuretic; improves digestion. Stimulates the uterus and reduces inflammation.

USES OF THE HERB:
Culinary
Add crushed berries to marinades for game and stuffings for poultry. Use whole berries to flavor pickles and sauerkraut. Add a few crushed berries to strong meats and game.

Cosmetic
Juniper oil extracted from pressed berries is used in spicy fragrances.

Medicinal
Take either the tincture or an infusion of juniper berries to ease cystitis. Applied as an oil, diluted first in a "carrier oil," juniper will also soothe aching muscles and rheumatic pains.

Household
The aroma of juniper essential oil is very pleasant and can be used in an oil burner to perfume the house. The berries are also used as part of potpourri.

CAUTION
Juniper berries should not be taken in quantity by people with a history of kidney problems or during early pregnancy. It is a very strong herb and should not be taken by the very ill or the elderly or by anybody for over three weeks continuously.

KAFFIR LIME

This thorny tropical tree is widely used in the Far East—the leaves and the juice of the fruit feature heavily in traditional stir-fries, curries, and soups. The fruit and its rind are used medicinally, and the extracted oil is used in toiletries.

In many respects, kaffir lime, or *Citrus hystrix*, resembles other citrus fruits—it is a member of the lemon family. *Hystrix* comes from the Greek word for porcupine—a reference to the large number of thorns on this tropical tree.

One of the best-known uses of kaffir lime is in the cookery of Southeast Asia, its original home. The leaves, with their sour taste and a fragrance reminiscent of lemon or lime peel, are especially popular in Thailand. Their pleasant, tangy flavor provides the distinctive flavor of many Thai soups, curries, and stir-fries. In Indonesian dishes, the leaves are added to fish and chicken. The sour juice of the kaffir lime fruits is also used in Southeast Asian cuisine—such as Philippine rice dishes, among others.

Funeral Rites

Traditionally, the flesh and juice of the limes have been used to promote a healthy, dandruff-free scalp and also in certain funeral rites in its native lands. During these rites, the fresh leaves are crushed and combined with other herbs to produce a fragrant water, which is then poured over the body or into the mouth. There has also been research into the possibility that the rind of the fruit might have some antifertility effect, as traditional Thai medicine uses it as an abortive agent. On the domestic front, the fruit pulp is also used by some Southeast Asian and Pacific peoples as a soap and shampoo and to wash clothes.

Thorny Tree

The kaffir lime is a variable evergreen tree with distinctive thorns. Its leaves—dark green above and paler below—are one to three inches long. Their stalks are often as large as the leaves. The tree's flowers grow in terminal clusters, and its green or green-yellow fruits are rounded, with flattened ends and warty or knobbly skin. This species should be grown like any other citrus. It needs regular feeding and watering during the growing season and must not be allowed to get waterlogged during winter.

Leaf
Distinctive, glossy wing-shaped leaves, dark on top and paler at the back.

Oriental Flavor
Green chicken curry, flavored with kaffir lime leaves, is a traditional dish from Thailand.

USES

PARTS USED:
Leaf, fruit, rind, juice, oil.

PROPERTIES:
Fragrant; tangy flavor; promotes a healthy scalp; may have antifertility effects.

USES OF THE HERB:
Culinary
The leaves and peel are popular in Southeast Asian cuisine.

Medicinal
The rind may have an abortive effect; fruits are used to clear flaky scalps.

Household
Traditionally used to wash clothes.

Cosmetic
Leaf oil is used in some citrus perfumes; the fruits are used as a traditional soap and shampoo.

LADY'S MANTLE

Not to be confused with the garden variety, also called "lady's mantle," this herb has medicinal uses unlike its namesake. It is a very bitter, astringent herb that controls bleeding and discharges.

As its name suggests, lady's mantle is a traditional healing herb for women—a natural astringent that is particularly useful for controlling bleeding or discharge. It may be taken internally for excessive or irregular menstruation, unpleasant menopausal symptoms, and vaginal itch or discharge.

Versatility
This herb is also useful in cases of diarrhea, and like its similar relation, *Alchemilla alpina* (alpine lady's mantle), can relieve the condition in animals as well as humans. The leaves may be made into a mouth rinse to be taken after tooth extraction. The leaves are edible, adding a bitter flavor to salads and yogurt, which is something of an acquired taste. They also yield a green dye suitable for wool, and the plant as a whole is excellent for flower arranging.

Preserving Youth
The generic name *Alchemilla* probably comes from the Arab word for alchemy—*alkemelych*—and the herb has certainly been credited over the centuries with magical healing properties. Women once washed in dew gathered from the leaves in May to preserve their youth and beauty, although this was only thought to work if they were naked and alone in the moonlight at the time.

Women's Remedy
During medieval times, lady's mantle was dedicated to the Virgin Mary and became a staple household remedy for various female ailments. In the eighteenth century, new mothers wrapped their breasts in the leaves to restore shape after breastfeeding.

Nowadays, this wild herb is usually cultivated as a pretty container plant, looking particularly attractive in a hanging basket. Its relative, *A. mollis*, also known as "lady's mantle," is a popular ornamental garden variety, cultivated for its foliage, but is not a medicinal plant. The dried flowers are popular in floral displays.

Stem
Hairy, upright to sprawling.

Leaf
Distinctly lobed but with an overall rounded shape and crinkled edges.

USES

PARTS USED:
Whole plant.

PROPERTIES:
Bitter, astringent; controls bleeding and discharges.

USES OF THE HERB:
Medicinal
Stems for bleeding and discharges. Taken internally for irregular or excessive menstrual bleeding and for menopausal symptoms. Used externally for vaginal discharge or itching. Also as a mouthwash after tooth extraction. Treatment for diarrhea (also in animals).

Culinary
Young leaves can be added to salads or yogurt, but this is not to everybody's taste.

Household
Boil leaves for a green wool dye.

Decorative
A good choice for flower arrangements.

LAVENDER

No garden is complete without lavender. A traditional cottage garden plant, it has always been appreciated for its sweet perfume, silver-gray foliage, and flowers in a variety of colors.

Lavender (from the Latin *lavare*, to wash) has long been valued for its fragrance and insect-repellent qualities. Centuries ago, lavender flowers were strewn on the floor to keep rooms freshly scented.

Lavender has also long been recognized as beneficial to the nervous system. Three hundred years ago, it was described as especially good for all forms of headache. Today, taken as an infusion, it will help a headache and conquer minor mental depression. It can be used to treat bruises, bites, and aches, and will lower blood pressure and calm palpitations. It is also antiseptic. To cure a migraine attack, draw a hot bath and add fifteen to twenty drops of lavender essential oil to it. Lie still in the bath for ten minutes, keeping the water hot. Then lie in a darkened room and try to sleep. When you wake, the pain should be gone. A few drops of essential oil in the bathwater will banish fatigue. A drop on the pillow of a restless child will help them to sleep.

Different Varieties

There are twenty-one varieties and many more hybrids. Colors vary from purple to white. English lavender (*Lavandula angustifolia*) is used in expensive perfumes since it yields a high-quality essential oil. A hybrid, lavendin (*L.* x *intermedia*), is widely grown for perfumery and as a garden plant. French or fringed lavender (*Lavandula dentata*) is also used in perfume. Spike lavender (*Lavandula latifolia*) is native to the Mediterranean and is the species most often used in cleaning products. It yields a very good oil for masking unpleasant smells.

USES

PARTS USED:
Flowers, oil.

PROPERTIES:
Aromatic, antiseptic, tonic herb, and sweet smelling.

USES OF THE HERB:
Culinary
Crystallize the flowers as decorations for cakes and puddings. Fresh flowers can also be added to jam or ice cream.

Medicinal
Take a weak infusion of the flowers for headaches and to lower blood pressure. Add lavender oil to a warm bath to help cure a migraine or aches and pains. The oil is an antiseptic and painkiller for bites and stings.

Cosmetic
Lavender mouthwash will help cure halitosis.

Household
Lavender is an insect repellent, so grow it near the patio. Sachets of dried lavender will keep away insects and also scent clothes. Useful in potpourri.

Decorative
Use in dried arrangements. Growing plants make a decorative hedge.

CAUTION
Do not use lavender if taking insulin for diabetes. Avoid in pregnancy.

Dried Flowers
Retain their clean, sweet scent for long periods.

Seeds
Gather small, dark brown seeds from the flower heads.

Leaf
Gray-green and narrow.

Stem
Square and green. Becomes woody in its second season.

LAWN CHAMOMILE

Flowering varieties of this plant have culinary and medicinal uses, while the nonflowering variety makes excellent ground cover, so much so that it can be cultivated to provide a fragrant lawn.

An aromatic, springy carpet of herbs makes an entrancing alternative to a conventional grass lawn. Among several herbs used for lawns, perhaps the most popular is chamomile (also known as "camomile"), immortalized in the novel *The Camomile Lawn*.

In fact, chamomile has been used for this purpose since medieval times. A seventeenth-century gardener wrote that it "delights the mind and brings health to the body." It grows well in warm, dry conditions, and the plants tolerate being walked on. As the leaves are crushed underfoot, they release a pleasant perfume, reminiscent of apples. The name actually derives from the Greek word *khamaimelon*, which means "apple on the ground." Although a chamomile lawn doesn't need mowing, it needs to be tended to prevent an invasion of weeds. It is best when bordered by either stones or bricks.

Choosing Varieties
Chamaemelum nobile is the best type for use as a lawn because it is low growing and spreads easily. The ideal choice is the nonflowering clone "Treneague," which forms a short, dense mat about one inch tall and remains green without attention. The flowering varieties will need the flower heads removed from time to time. However, lack of flowers means that this clone cannot be used as a medicinal or culinary herb because it is the flowers of chamomile that have these properties.

Other Options
Instead of a chamomile lawn, which can be difficult to maintain over a large area, there are other ways to make the most of this plant. Plant it in containers or in gaps in paving. It can also be used in a raised area to create an outdoor "seat." Another option is a chamomile path winding through an herb garden—the scent can be enjoyed and the leaves dried to use in potpourri and herbal pillows.

Leaf
Feathery, bright green leaves give off an apple scent when crushed.

Seeds
Ordinary chamomile can be grown from seed, but the preferred clone, "Treneague," must be propagated by division.

USES

PARTS USED:
Whole plant, leaves, and flowers.

PROPERTIES:
A fragrant herb with culinary and medicinal uses that also provides good ground cover.

USES OF THE HERB:
Culinary
Use flowering varieties for herbal drinks.

Medicinal
The flowers can be used to make an infusion. Use as a lotion to soothe sore or irritated skin and as a mild sedative tea for insomnia.

Household
The presence of chamomile in the garden will often help to revive ailing nearby plants. The aromatic leaves can be picked for use in potpourri and herbal pillows.

LEMON BALM

This fragrant garden plant releases its scent when brushed against. It is also widely used in the kitchen and for its medicinal effects.

Lemon balm should be a first choice for the herb garden since it is both decorative and useful. Its pleasant lemon-scented leaves should be placed where they can be brushed against, releasing their delightful fragrance. The plant takes its name from the Greek word for honeybee—*melissa*—and is highly attractive to bees, who were believed never to leave any garden in which it was grown. In days gone by, before sugar was widely available, honey was highly prized, and this was an important consideration. During the Middle Ages, lemon balm was widely used for strewing on floors since it possessed the important qualities of smelling pleasant and driving insects away.

Cheering Spirits
Lemon balm has long been established as one of the most effective herbs in banishing depression. Five hundred years ago, it was called "the elixir of life," and during the eighteenth century, it was taken to renew vigor. Lemon balm tea was claimed to have been drunk by several people who lived to be over one hundred years old.

An infusion of lemon balm is excellent for calming nerves, and a cup taken at bedtime will aid sleep. It is also good for menstrual cramps. Tea is much more effective if it is made from fresh, rather than dried, leaves.

Lemon balm flowers are insignificant—the plant is grown primarily for its foliage. The ornamental varieties can look marvelous in a flower bed. They include the variegated "Aurea," which contains a splash of yellow, and the "All Gold" variety, which is entirely yellow.

Leaf
Deep-veined leaves have a strong lemon scent. They prefer light shade—full sun may turn them yellow and reduce their scent.

USES

PARTS USED:
Whole plant, leaves, and oil.

PROPERTIES:
An aromatic, cooling, and sedative herb; lowers fever and relaxes spasms; also antibacterial and antiviral, and acts as an insect repellent.

USES OF THE HERB:
Culinary
Chop the leaves into salad. Add to fruit salads, jams, ice cream, and custard. Add to blended vinegars. The leaves can be crystallized and added to cakes. Can also be added to game and fish.

Cosmetic
Infuse as a hair rinse or add to bath water to give a delicious scent.

Decorative
Use the leaves in potpourri.

Medicinal
Good for feverish colds, nervousness, and depression, including baby blues after childbirth. Add a cupful of infusion to a bath for a fretful baby or hyperactive child. Good remedy for childhood infections and chronic bronchitis. Use lemon balm oil externally on cold sores.

Household
Crush fresh leaves and rub onto bee or wasp stings for a soothing and healing effect. You can make lemon balm tinctures and ointments for year-round use. Put a few drops of the essential oil in an oil burner to repel insects. Oil can be added to furniture polish for a sweet smell.

Dried Leaf
Dried lemon balm loses some of its scent and medicinal properties.

LEMONGRASS

This fragrant herb is a versatile one—it is widely used as a flavoring ingredient in Southeast Asian dishes and has a range of medicinal applications as well.

Wherever you site lemongrass plants, make sure that it is in a place where you can press the long, vivid green leaves as you walk past. This will release the fresh lemon scent for which this herb is famous and which adds so much fragrance or flavor to products as diverse as fish dishes, perfume, potpourri, and confectionery.

There are over fifty species in this genus of scented grasses, native to tropical and temperate regions of the world and to the grassy plains of Sri Lanka and southern India. Plants can be grown outdoors in warmer areas and will happily survive the warmer months outside in cool areas, as long as they are brought indoors when the temperature falls below 45°F.

Cymbopogon grasses either contain citral, which is a lemon fragrance, as in *C. citratus*, or geraniol, which gives a rose scent, as in the species *C. martinii*. Usually found growing in distinctive clumps, the long, thin leaves can reach great lengths in the right conditions. The plant seldom produces flowers.

A Variety of Uses

This is a bitter herb with cooling and calming properties. The leaves, stem, and oil are the valuable parts of the plant. Only the lower four inches of the leaves are really suitable for use—fresh or dried, in teas and Oriental or Asian cookery. To use the stems, cut them off above ground level and use either fresh or dried. The stems are also a rich source of an aromatic oil, which is commercially extracted. The oil finds its way into all kinds of household and cosmetic products, lending them a highly distinctive fragrance, and features as a popular flavoring in a variety of foods. The lemongrass oil commonly sold for flavoring purposes is taken from the species *C. flexuosus* (East Indian lemongrass).

Stem
Strong stem is reminiscent of cane. Base of stem is sliced and used for culinary purposes.

Adding Zest
Lemongrass features strongly in Thai cooking, its sharp, fresh flavor predominating in dishes such as fragrant rice and red and green curries.

USES

PARTS USED:
Leaves, stems, and oil.

PROPERTIES:
Aromatic, bitter, calming, and cooling; antifungal and antibacterial.

USES OF THE HERB:
Culinary
The fresh or dried leaf bases add a distinctive character to Southeast Asian fish and meat dishes. Chop young stems into salads. Can also be used in powder form.

Medicinal
This herb's antibacterial and antifungal properties help combat conditions such as athlete's foot; its cooling, calming properties relieve fever by promoting perspiration. Can also help children's digestive upsets.

Household
Add to scented sachets and potpourri.

Cosmetic
Lemongrass oil is used in cosmetics, soap, and perfume—use it to cleanse oily skin or add to a bath.

Decorative
This aromatic herb gives a refreshing boost to potpourri.

LEMON VERBENA

This fragrant herb makes an attractive feature in a mixed border. It is also indispensable in the kitchen, especially for herbal teas, and is used medicinally and in a variety of cosmetics.

As its name suggests, lemon verbena is best known for the strong citrus aroma of its leaves. South American in origin, it is relatively easy to grow and is widely cultivated in many other regions for its foliage and as a source of essential oil, which has antibacterial and insecticidal properties. Aromatherapists use its essential oil to treat digestive problems and nervous complaints and the plant's astringent qualities to combat acne, boils, and cysts. Leaf infusions can be good for colds and fever and act as a gentle sedative and antispasmodic.

Lemon verbena leaves are picked in summer and used fresh in herbal teas and in syrups, salads, or stuffing for meat and poultry. They can also be chopped and sprinkled over drinks and fruit desserts. When dried, they hold their fragrance for several years—making them ideal for potpourri or herbal sachets. A strained infusion of the leaves or flowers also makes a refreshing final rinse for laundry, or may be added to a warm bath to produce an invigorating effect.

Household Scent
Lemon verbena was introduced to Europe toward the end of the eighteenth century—the genus, *Aloysia*, was named after the Italian princess, Maria Louisa of Parma, who died in 1819. In Victorian England, *Aloysia triphylla* was known simply as "the lemon plant," and its clean, sharp fragrance made it very popular around the home. It was heavily cultivated by the Spanish for its valuable oil, much used by perfumiers.

Cultivation
This South American native is common in fields and on grass verges in Argentina and Chile. When cultivated in cooler climates, it is normally frost-hardy, but prefers a warm, sheltered spot. It produces pale purple flowers, but its main feature is its foliage, which is most aromatic in the early evening.

USES

PARTS USED:
Leaves, oil.

PROPERTIES:
Aromatic, astringent; rich in volatile oils; mild sedative; relieves spasms, especially of the digestive system; reduces fever; oil is insecticidal and antibacterial.

USES OF THE HERB:
Culinary
Add fresh leaves to herb teas, salads, and stuffing for meat and poultry. Finely chop leaves to flavor drinks and fruit desserts.

Medicinal
Astringent, sedative, and antispasmodic. Essential oil used for digestive problems, nervous complaints, acne, boils, and cysts. Infusions for colds and fever.

Cosmetic
Perfume, skin, and hair preparations.

Household
Use dried leaves in potpourri, herbal pillows, and sachets, or as an infusion as a final laundry rinse.

CAUTION
Lemon verbena essential oil may sensitize the skin to sunlight.

Stem
Round and ridged. Green but later turns reddish and woody.

Leaf
Long and pointed, with a strong lemony scent, especially when crushed.

Flower
Loose spikes of tiny white or pale purple flowers appear in summer.

Dried Leaves
The dried leaves retain their fragrance well, making them ideal for potpourri.

LICORICE

This tall herb is most familiar for the sweet black confectionery made from it, but it also has a wide range of medicinal uses.

Leaf
Sticky leaves with leaflets arranged on either side of the stem.

Licorice Root
The licorice root is processed to provide various forms that are used in confectionery and medicines.

Roots and Runners
Crushed and boiled to extract juice and produce a sweet, black paste.

Sweet Treats
The familiar substance used in black licorice sweets is extracted by boiling the roots to produce a sweet paste.

Licorice is perhaps most familiar as confectionery, but its sweet-tasting roots and runners have a host of other properties. Known for its purifying effect on the liver and spleen, this herb is often used as an anti-inflammatory, as it contains glycyrrhizin, a highly sweet substance that acts like the steroid hormone cortisone.

Licorice root can be used to treat all kinds of ailments, from asthma and Addison's disease (a disease of the hormone system) to arthritis and allergies. Externally, licorice can be used for complaints such as cold sores, eczema, and shingles. Ayurvedic practitioners prescribe it for ulcers, malaria, and throat infections. It is, however, harmful if taken in excess.

The black substance extracted from the roots and used in confectionery also makes a good base for laxatives and other medicines. It flavors soft drinks and features as a foaming agent in fire extinguishers. It is also used in shoe polish.

Pontefract Cakes
Glycyrrhiza glabra was prominent in ancient Egypt, Assyria, and China, and was prescribed for asthma and dry coughs during the time of the early Greek physician Dioscorides.

Healing Species
Several near relations are also important medicinal herbs. In America, *Glycyrrhiza lepidota* was used as a folk remedy by natives and early settlers to ease problems with menstruation. Chinese, or Manchurian, licorice (*Glycyrrhiza uralensis*) is known in Chinese medicine as *gan cao*, and is often used for its sweet flavor, being combined with less palatable plants. Three variants of *Glycyrrhiza glabra*—*typica* (Spanish or Italian licorice), *violacea* (Persian or Turkish), and *glandulifera* (Russian)—also have medicinal value.

USES

PARTS USED:
Roots, stolons (runners).

PROPERTIES:
Soothing, anti-inflammatory, anti-viral, antibacterial, and expectorant; hormonal effects; protects liver.

USES OF THE HERB:
Culinary
Used to flavor sweets and soft drinks.

Medicinal
Detoxifies liver and spleen, and taken internally for asthma, Addison's disease, bronchitis, coughs, peptic ulcers, arthritis, allergies, and follow-up to steroids. Externally for cold sores, eczema, and shingles. Chewing the root can combat constipation.

CAUTION
Can raise blood pressure, cause water retention, and act as laxative. Not to be taken during pregnancy or by patients with high blood pressure. Should only be used under expert guidance.

LOVAGE

This single species occurs naturally in the eastern Mediterranean region. The new celery-scented growth appears in early spring when few other culinary herbs are available.

This well-loved plant, commonly known as lovage, is a traditional feature of the garden. It is in fact a native of Iran and flourishes in warm Balkan and Mediterranean regions. This tall and leafy species, with a powerful aroma and sweetish flavor that is strongly reminiscent of celery, was once popular in the kitchen but fell out of favor as a culinary herb. Lovage is now gaining popularity once again.

All parts of the plant can be used. Fresh young leaves and seeds can be added to salads, while young stems and shoots can be used like celery—cooked as a vegetable or as an ingredient in soups, casseroles, and stews.

The aromatic properties of lovage give it a host of other uses too. The fragrant seeds can be added to potpourri, while leafy stems look attractive and smell pleasant as a part of floral arrangements. Medicinally, lovage eases spasms and has a diuretic effect. An infusion, especially of the roots, but also of the leaves and seeds, can be taken to ease a range of problems, especially indigestion, gas, stomach ache, and urinary disorders, such as cystitis. Lovage extracts and oil are used commercially to flavor a variety of foods as well as drinks, and the oil is also used in perfumery.

Cultivation

This species—the only one in its genus—is extremely hardy and robust, so it is a good choice for most gardens, grown in fertile, moist soil. It should not be confused with plants in the genus *Ligusticum*, which are referred to commonly as various types of lovage. For example, *Ligusticum scoticum*, or "Scots lovage," also has a celery-like aroma and taste and similar properties and uses to *Levisticum officinale*.

USES

PARTS USED:
Leaves, seeds, stems, roots.

PROPERTIES:
Aromatic, bittersweet, diuretic, expectorant, and sedative; aids digestion, increases perspiration, and relaxes spasms.

USES OF THE HERB:
Culinary
Cook stems and roots as a vegetable; use stems, roots, and leaves in soups and casseroles. Add young leaves, seeds, and grated root to salads.

Medicinal
Relaxes digestive system and helps to relieve cystitis, bronchitis, mouth ulcers, and menstrual cramps.

Cosmetic
Use an infusion of seeds, leaves, or roots as a deodorant, facial wash, or cleansing addition to a bath.

Decorative
Use leafy stems in flower arrangements.

CAUTION
Do not use in pregnancy; not to be taken by those with kidney problems.

Leaf
The large leaves resemble those of the celery plant and also taste and smell similar to celery.

Seeds
Brown, crescent-shaped seeds have a celery-like aroma.

Stem
Round, hollow, and ridged stems are celery-like and branch toward the top.

Dried Leaves
The dried leaves can be used to make a pleasant celery-flavored herbal tea to ease indigestion.

LUNGWORT

With its spotted variegated leaves and delicate flowers, lungwort is a garden favorite. As its name indicates, its medicinal uses are related to the respiratory system.

Flower
Bell-like blooms produced between March and May. Pinkish at first, then slowly turn blue or mauve as they open fully.

Stem
Stem covered with hairs.

Leaf
Oval, alternate, hairy leaves are variegated with distinctive silver-white spots.

Ground Cover
With its pretty spring flowers and spotted foliage, lungwort looks especially attractive planted either as ground cover or in clumps at the edge of borders.

The curious common name "soldiers and sailors" that has been used for this plant springs from its unusual blooms, which begin their life pink or reddish and turn blue or mauve as they open. At one time, these were the colors of soldiers' and sailors' uniforms. These multicolored blooms last through the spring. The young and tender leaves of this species can be added to salads. As a therapeutic herb, the plant is known chiefly for easing problems related to the lungs—coughs, catarrh, and bronchial congestion—which is how the name lungwort came into being (*pulmo* is the Latin word for "lung").

Doctrine of Signatures

Lungwort has long been associated with the treatment of lung complaints, and this owes a great deal to the fact that its spotted leaves were thought to look like diseased lungs. During the 1500s, a very influential school of thought called the Doctrine of Signatures gained credence in Europe. This was based around the idea that herbs resembled the complaints that they were supposed to help. The plant contains various substances, including saponins, silicic acid, mucilage, bitters, and vitamin C, that do, in fact, help with conditions involving the respiratory system.

Variegated Low-grower

Lungwort is low growing, and its attractive spotted foliage makes it a good choice for ground cover. It should not be confused with the species *Lobaria pulmonaria*, a lichen, which is also known as lungwort.

Although famed by gardeners for its multicolored pink and blue flowers, this species is also available in a white semievergreen form: *P. officinalis* "Sissinghurst White," which is early flowering and grows vigorously to about twelve inches tall. A native of woodlands and thickets, lungwort prefers a shady spot but is happy in most types of soil with a good supply of moisture. It can be propagated from seed, but germination can take time; plants can be divided in spring or autumn. The foliage may be attacked by sawfly larvae.

USES

PARTS USED:
Flowering plant.

PROPERTIES:
Astringent, expectorant, diuretic, and soothing.

USES OF THE HERB:
Medicinal
Leaves and stems are expectorant and diuretic. Infusions help coughs, sore throats, catarrh, chest congestion, and an aching neck. Also taken for diarrhea, hemorrhoids, and small wounds and to control bleeding.

Culinary
Use young leaves in salads.

Decorative
Makes a handsome garden plant.

CAUTION
Tests show that lungwort, like comfrey (*Symphytum officinale*), contains alkaloids that, in very large doses, have been found to cause liver damage in animals. It is subject to legal restrictions in some countries.

MANDRAKE

Fuel for a witch's broomstick and a history just as long, mandrake's past is colored by sorcery and black magic. More prosaically, it is used as a sedative and painkiller.

Flower
White or pale blue-white; bell shaped with five petals. Borne in spring.

Leaf
Large, dark green, oval leaves.

Root
Stout, brown taproot, often shaped like the human body, reaches deep underground.

The Mediterranean herb mandrake has a long and colorful history steeped in tales of superstition, black magic, and sorcery. The image of witches on broomsticks may have originated from the use of mandrake and other plants, which give a sensation of flying. Many of these tales no doubt spring from the shape and medicinal properties of its forked root, thought to resemble the human form.

Sedative
Mandrake is certainly dangerous to use at home since it is also a powerful narcotic and poison that should only be used under medical supervision. It was once employed as a natural sedative and painkiller for patients about to undergo surgery, and the active alkaloid hyoscine is still extracted from the roots and put to the same use today.

Ulcer Treatment
Mandrake can also trigger therapeutic purging and vomiting and is sometimes prescribed by homeopathic practitioners. It may be applied externally to ulcers.

Devil's Apples
Mandrake's common and Latin names both spring from the Greek word *mandra*, which means a stall or herd of cattle and is probably a reference to the harm it could cause livestock if eaten. Some believe the name is derived from the Assyrian *nam tar ira*, meaning "male drug of Namtar," reflecting its reputation as a fertility aid. It was also widely known as "devil's apples" on account of its round, yellow fruit and chilling associations with sorcery.

Screaming Roots
In ancient and medieval times, it was thought that mandrakes would scream if uprooted, frightening anyone in the vicinity, literally, to death—hence the tradition of tying a dog to the root to do the work. The herb was also said to have the power to free a person possessed by demons. Despite these associations with the occult, mandrake was mostly used for medicinal purposes and became an official homeopathic remedy in 1877. It is sometimes grown in the garden for its novelty value.

USES

PARTS USED:
Roots.

PROPERTIES:
Painkilling, sedative; purgative and emetic effects.

USES OF THE HERB:
Medicinal
Sedative (especially pre-operative) and painkiller. Triggers vomiting. Homeopathic remedy, formerly taken for nervous conditions and as a fertility aid. Applied externally to ulcers. Combats motion sickness.

CAUTION
Poisonous narcotic—should not be used at home. Medicinal use subject to legal restrictions in some countries. Do not confuse with American mandrake (*Podophyllum peltatum*).

Flower
Measures 2–3 in. across, with daisy-like radiating petals. Can be used to color and flavor many foods.

Seeds
About ¼ in. long and C-shaped. Light to mid brown when ripe.

Dried Marigold Petals
Dried marigold is sold for making infusions, coloring, and flavoring food and for medicinal uses.

Leaf
Mid green and fleshy. Occasionally used in salads and stews.

MARIGOLD

As well as its vibrant flowers, which can be seen in gardens for most of the summer, this plant has many other uses—both culinary and medicinal, including the treatment of skin conditions.

More often cultivated for its eye-catching flowers than for its practical uses, this colorful herb blooms almost continuously. The decorative flowers are a bright yellow-orange, bringing year-round sunshine and life to the garden. The Romans believed that the marigold could be found in flower on the first of every month and called it *calendula*, Latin for "calendar." Planted in the garden, marigold will also keep many insect pests away from other flowers. But it has many practical uses in the kitchen and home, as well as in medicine.

Powerful Medicine
Five hundred years ago, marigold was a great favorite of King Henry VIII, who mixed it with sorrel, feverfew, snapdragon, and rue, believing it would combat the plague. Herbalists of King Henry's time used it in the treatment of smallpox, but while it may have helped, its main uses are to reduce inflammation and accelerate healing.

During World War I, marigold was used extensively in the trenches in order to prevent sepsis and to clean filthy wounds. It proved to be invaluable in a situation where there was a shortage of medical supplies. There is also evidence that marigold was used by surgeons during the Civil War. Nowadays it is available as an ointment or tincture and as a homeopathic remedy. It benefits all problems relating to the skin including eczema, bruising, diaper rash, and minor burns.

USES

PARTS USED:
Flower petals.

PROPERTIES:
Stimulates the uterus, gallbladder, and liver; clears infections and is beneficial to the skin.

USES OF THE HERB:
Culinary
Use marigold leaves in salads and stews. Add the petals to fish dishes and salads. Marigold can also be used as coloring for rice.

Medicinal
Drink an infusion to heal wounds in the digestive tract, such as ulcers and colitis. It also helps the lymphatic system and can aid swollen glands. Use it for viral and fungal infections such as thrush and athlete's foot. An infusion in a bath will help heal and clean an injury.

Household
Use to add color to potpourri.

Cosmetic
Infuse as a face wash and a hair rinse for auburn hair. Use as an eye bath to soothe tired, itchy eyes.

CAUTION
Do not confuse the plant with wild marsh marigold, which is mildly poisonous, or with French marigold (*Tagetes*), which has different uses. Do not drink infusions in pregnancy or when breastfeeding.

MATÉ

This evergreen tree is popular in South America, where its dried leaves are used to make a drink. It is also a stimulant and diuretic.

The evergreen tree known as maté is a native of scrubland and forest in South America, especially in Paraguay. One of its other common names is "Paraguay tea"—Paraguay is one of the main countries in which this tree is found. The *Ilex* genus as a whole is better known as holly—a highly popular and variable group of plants that favor the milder and tropical regions of the world. Holly, especially the common species *Ilex aquifolium*, is perhaps best known in the Western world as a traditional form of decoration at Christmas, but certain hollies are used both in drinks and medicinally.

Native American Cure
Maté, a highly popular drink in South America, has a range of popular therapeutic uses, dating back to the traditional medicine of the Native Americans. The drink, with its painkilling and stimulant properties, is taken for tension headaches, depression, and nerve pain. Maté is known to be a diuretic—large doses can have a strongly purgative effect, causing vomiting in some cases. It is also reputed to be an appetite suppressant.

Cultivation
This shrub is cultivated for its leaves and should be kept well trimmed. It prefers moist soil and warm temperatures and does not tolerate frost. The leafy shoots are collected throughout the year and dried for use in various infusions. Maté may be damaged by leaf spot or holly leaf miner and dislikes root disturbance. The berries are harmful if ingested.

USES

PARTS USED:
Leaves.

PROPERTIES:
Stimulant, pain reliever, diuretic, antispasmodic; clears toxins.

USES OF THE HERB:
Medicinal
Taken internally, as a tea, to ease muscular spasms and the pain of nerve conditions such as neuralgia; **clear the body of toxins; and help tension headaches, migraines, and depression (not severe or chronic).**

CAUTION
Excess can cause vomiting. Berries are poisonous if eaten.

Leaf
Large, oval, alternate leaves have distinctively scalloped edge.

Stem
Straight, gray-green with alternating leaves.

MINT

There are many varieties of mint; all have a distinctive, but not identical, smell and appearance in common. The common garden mint is perhaps the most widely appreciated as it can be put to so many varied uses.

It has been said that mint is the most popular flavoring in the world—appearing in so many foodstuffs and medicines that it is often barely given a second thought. There are many varieties of mint, but the one that appears in the majority of gardens is *Mentha spicata*, also known as "spearmint"—the taste that is commonly associated with chewing gum and toothpaste. The different types of mint are rich sources of various volatile oils, but all contain menthol, which provides the characteristic smell and taste.

Spearmint—which is milder in taste and aroma than peppermint, the other highly popular mint—is a stimulating herb that is both cooling and warming. It can be extremely effective in easing spasms, hiccups, indigestion, and gas, and easily taken as a pleasant herbal tea. Spearmint is also recommended for lowering certain fevers. As a culinary herb, it is traditionally used in tabbouleh, a Middle Eastern dish of vegetables and burgul (cracked wheat), and in Greek tzatziki, with yogurt, cucumber, and garlic. Commercially, it is used to flavor chewing gum, confectionery, and a range of oral hygiene products.

Herbal Wisdom

Spearmint has been valued as a culinary herb since the days of ancient Rome. It is now an important commercial crop, grown for its leaves and oil.

This hardy, creeping perennial can easily become rampant, so restrict it by growing it in a container (which can be sunk beneath the surface of the soil). It should be divided and repotted each year when dormant, and dead stems cut back in the autumn. Spikes of tiny flowers appear during the summer and early autumn. It can be grown from seed or cuttings and grows best in moist soil. It prefers partial shade rather than full sun.

Leaves
Bright green, lance-shaped leaves have a spearmint aroma, little or no stalk, strongly marked veins, and toothed edges.

New Potatoes
Served with fresh mint, a culinary classic that combines well with meat dishes.

Chopped Fresh Mint
Freshly chopped mint is used extensively as a flavoring ingredient in the kitchen—it is particularly popular with lamb and potato dishes.

USES

PARTS USED:
Whole plant, leaves.

PROPERTIES:
A stimulating herb, both cooling and warming; contains volatile oils, including menthol.

USES OF THE HERB:
Culinary
Use spearmint in salads and a number of other dishes, and use as an attractive garnish on desserts.

Medicinal
The cooling, warming, and stimulating effects of this herb make it effective in relieving digestive problems and soothing fevers.

Household
Added to scented candles, mint produces a stimulating aroma with hints of caraway, which comes from a substance called "carvone" found in spearmint.

Decorative
Include in floral arrangements and wreaths to produce a clean, fresh scent.

MISTLETOE

The Druids, an ancient order of Celtic priests, used mistletoe as a fertility symbol and to welcome in the new year. It is also mentioned in Scandinavian mythology.

Famous as the plant under which couples kiss during the Christmas season, mistletoe is a parasitic evergreen shrub found growing on deciduous hosts, such as apple and hawthorn trees. The scientific name *Viscum* comes from the Latin word meaning both "mistletoe" and "birdlime"—the plant's active ingredient is a resin called "viscin," which ferments to form a sticky substance that was once spread on branches to catch small birds. The other major use of this bittersweet plant is as a medical remedy. Its leaves and stems have a strong numbing effect on hyperactive organs, calming fits and fevers as well as preventing hardening of the arteries and reducing blood pressure and nervous tension. As an external poultice, the plant has been used successfully in cases of rheumatism, arthritis, leg ulcers, and chilblains, as well as varicose veins. It is also used to treat lung and ovarian cancers.

Fertility Symbol

Mistletoe was sacred to the ancient Druids, who cut it from host trees at certain stages of the moon's cycle with a special golden knife and believed that it would protect them from evil. It was also considered a symbol of fertility, which is probably how couples came to kiss beneath it at Christmas. Scandinavian legend tells how Balder, god of peace, was killed with an arrow made from the shrub. In the 1600s and 1700s, medical texts extolled the virtues of mistletoe as a cure for epileptic spasms—paradoxically, eating the toxic fruits can actually result in convulsive fits.

Chosen Hosts

There are over seventy species within the *Viscum* genus, all evergreen parasites. *Viscum album* itself varies slightly, depending on its host. It produces unremarkable yellow flowers during the spring that are followed by toxic single-seeded berries. The shrub can be propagated by crushing the ripe fruits and pressing them into cracks in the bark of likely host trees during spring.

Stem
Smooth, green-brown stem is pendulous and regularly branched.

Leaf
Thick, leathery, yellow-green leaves are broadly tongue-shaped.

Fruit
Sticky white fruits are poisonous if eaten.

USES

PARTS USED:
Leaves and stems.

PROPERTIES:
Bittersweet, diuretic, pungent, and warming; anticancer effects; lowers blood pressure, slows heartbeat, stimulates immune system, and calms spasms.

USES OF THE HERB:
Medicinal
This warming plant has both stimulating and sedative actions. It is also thought to have some effect against certain types of cancer. Mistletoe is used externally to treat arthritis, rheumatism, and leg ulcers. Not to be used without professional guidance.

Decorative
Mistletoe is a traditional Christmas plant, hung up in sprigs to bring good fortune.

CAUTION
Use as a remedy under professional guidance only—all parts of the plant may be poisonous if eaten. The sale of mistletoe as a medical remedy is restricted in certain parts of the world.

Leaf
Deeply divided with prominent veins. Dull green in color with a strong smell. Up to 3 in. long. The basal leaves are a different shape.

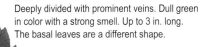

Flower
White or pinkish-mauve with purple spots on the lip; downy surface. Appear in whorls in leaf axils from midsummer to mid-autumn; calyx prickly.

Stem
Purple, reaching a height of 4 ft.

Dried
Motherwort has long been used in folk medicine. It is taken for its sedative properties and to treat palpitations and menstrual problems.

MOTHERWORT

This herb has a long tradition as a folk remedy—it was used by the ancient Greeks to calm pregnant women and to treat "women's problems." It is also prescribed for some heart conditions and has other medicinal applications.

This herb is distinctive both in appearance and in smell. Its deeply cut foliage makes a good backdrop for other herbs in the garden, and it has also been cultivated over the centuries for use in folk medicine. As its Latin name suggests, *Leonurus cardiaca* is associated with the heart. It is a natural sedative, widely prescribed for palpitations and also proven to help ward off thrombosis.

Extremely bitter in taste, it stimulates the circulation in general and helps to lower blood pressure. Motherwort also acts on the uterus—hence its connection with women's health. It is diuretic, antispasmodic, and fights fungal and bacterial infection.

Motherwort gets its common name from ancient Greece, where it was employed to calm pregnant women. All four species of *Leonurus*—ranging throughout temperate Eurasia—are believed to have similar properties. *Leonurus cardiaca* is often grown for its dramatic foliage, as is its more easterly relative, *L. sibiricus* (Chinese motherwort), a native of Siberia, China, Korea, and Taiwan. *Leonorus sibiricus* can be found in the *Illustrated Classic of the Materia Medica*, written by Su Song at the start of the second century AD. Known as *yi mu cao*, it is often prescribed on its own, which is unusual in Chinese medicine.

"Gladdening the Heart"
Leonurus cardiaca has a long history as a European household remedy. Mrs. M. Grieve remarks in her book *A Modern Herbal*, "Old writers tell us that there is no better herb for strengthening and gladdening the heart." Motherwort is relatively easy to grow in the garden and will soon spread. It can tolerate many kinds of soil, including stony ground.

USES

PARTS USED:
Whole plant.

PROPERTIES:
The whole plant is sedative, diuretic, and antispasmodic, and fights fungal and bacterial infection. It stimulates the circulation and the uterus.

USES OF THE HERB:
Medicinal
Internally for palpitations and other heart complaints, and problems

linked to menstruation, childbirth, and menopause.

CAUTION
No longer prescribed during pregnancy.

MYRRH

This ancient aromatic plant was used throughout the Middle and Far East for its exotic perfume. It acts as a stimulant and expectorant among other medicinal properties.

The word "myrrh" instantly conjures up the exotic perfumes and incenses of the Middle East, as well as the biblical tale of the precious gifts brought to the infant Jesus by the three wise men. Myrrh is a pungently aromatic oleo-gum-resin that oozes from several species of shrubs and trees of the *Commiphora* genus. Highly drought-resistant, these are found across the world's arid semideserts, from South America to the Middle East, Africa, and India. Widely used is the spiny shrub *Commiphora myrrha*, commonly known as myrrh.

Medicinal Myrrh
Famed for its use in perfumes and incenses, myrrh resin has a range of medicinal uses. This is a potent remedy—astringent, tonic, stimulating, expectorant, healing, and strongly antiseptic. The dried resin is processed so that it can be prescribed as oil, tablets, or a tincture. It is taken to ease digestive, bronchial, and menstrual disorders, and to heal wounds, as well as for a range of infections such as tonsillitis and mouth ulcers. It is included in many oral hygiene products. Myrrh combines well with other herbs, for example with wild thyme (*Thymus serpyllum*) to ease throat infections.

Middle Eastern Promise
Myrrh probably originated in the Middle East and is strongly linked with the history and sacred practices of that region—burning myrrh in incense was a standard purification ritual. Myrrh also burned in the temples of many other great civilizations, from ancient Egypt—where it was used for embalming—to ancient India. It became a highly valuable trading substance across much of the world.

Collecting Resin
Myrrh has been a traditional remedy in the Middle East since biblical times and in India and China for thousands of years. Today, resin is still gathered in the wild. It collects in fissures in the shrub or tree bark and is yellow when molten, drying to a reddish-brown. After the rains, the myrrh shrub brightens its arid surroundings by bursting into flower—the flowers are yellowish red and have four petals.

USES

PARTS USED:
Oleo-gum-resin.

PROPERTIES:
Aromatic, astringent, antiseptic, expectorant, pungent, stimulant, antispasmodic, and anti-inflammatory; aids digestion.

USES OF THE HERB:
Medicinal
Established in the Middle East for thousands of years as a purifying remedy, and used for poor digestion, catarrhal and bronchial disorders, wounds, and menstrual problems.

Healing, antiseptic properties aid conditions such as mouth ulcers, tonsillitis, and ear infections. An ingredient of oral hygiene products such as toothpaste.

Household
Crystals mixed with oil and scent-fixing gum can be burnt to fragrance a room.

Leaf
Small leaves made up of oval leaflets.

Stem
Stem and knotted branches yield aromatic oleo-gum-resin. Small branches end in a spine.

Joss Sticks
Its pungent scent has made myrrh popular in joss sticks. Other fragrant powdered herbs, such as lavender and sandalwood, are sometimes included to create an even more exotic aromatic scent.

Resin Nuggets
Lumps of dried resin are oily, semi-transparent, brittle, and granular, with a rough surface.

Flower
Single, fragrant, white, five-petaled flowers with numerous golden stamens. Around 1¼ in. across.

Leaf
Lustrous, oval, dark green leaves. Juniper aroma.

Stem
Upright, slender, reddish-brown, and woody.

MYRTLE

Long associated with the ancient love goddesses, myrtle is still used as a romantic symbol in wedding bouquets. It also has both culinary and medicinal applications.

This pretty, evergreen native of southwestern Europe and the Mediterranean has been valued as a culinary and medicinal herb since ancient times. The aromatic leaves are particularly suited to Mediterranean and Middle Eastern cuisine and are used to flavor dishes of pork, lamb, and small birds. In the Middle East, the fruits, or *mursins*, are used as a spice. Myrtle oil, distilled from the whole plant, is widely used by perfumiers. It is also an ingredient in toiletries such as soap and skin preparations. As far back as the sixteenth century, the flowers were distilled to make *eau d'ange*, a popular skin tonic. Various parts of the plant are dried for use in herbal medicine, and its active chemical compounds are quickly absorbed by the body. Taken internally, it can help to clear urinary infections and vaginal discharge, as well as coughs, sinusitis, and bronchial congestion. Externally, it treats hemorrhoids and gum disease, and the oil is used to treat acne.

Symbol of Love
Myrtle is also a traditional symbol of love—it is still a common feature of wedding bouquets in the Middle East and in the UK royal family. It was dedicated to Venus, the Roman goddess of love, who is often shown wearing a myrtle crown and who was sometimes referred to as "Myrtilla," from the herb's Latin name. Myrtle had similar associations for the ancient Greeks, being sacred to their goddess of love, Aphrodite. It was also linked with Ishtar, the Babylonian and Assyrian goddess of love and fertility. Other fables abound—the ancient Jews, for example, held that anyone who ate myrtle leaves would be able to detect witches.

Dwarf Myrtle
There are several cultivars of myrtle, all of which make lovely container plants but need a warm spot such as a sunny wall or patio. Myrtle can reach ten feet in height, so in small gardens where space may be limited, the dwarf *M. communis* subsp. *tarentina* is a good option. The attractive cultivar *M. communis* "Flore Pleno" has long-lasting, double white flowers and can grow to a height of fifteen feet. *Myrtus communis* "Variegat" has attractive foliage but is less hardy.

USES

PARTS USED:
Leaves, fruit, whole plant, oil.

PROPERTIES:
Aromatic, astringent, and antiseptic; decongestant.

USES OF THE HERB:
Medicinal
Astringent, antiseptic, and decongestant. Taken internally for urinary infections and vaginal discharge, coughs, sinusitis, and bronchial congestion (urine takes on scent of violets). External use for acne (oil), hemorrhoids, and gum disease.

Culinary
Leaves and dried berries used in Mediterranean and Middle Eastern cuisine; good with pork and lamb.

Cosmetic
Plant commercially distilled for oil used in perfume, soap, and skin products. Flowers distilled for *eau d'ange*.

Decorative
Ancient symbol of love—used in wedding bouquets.

NETTLE

Regarded as a weed, this plant with its stinging leaves is usually gathered in the wild. It grows readily on waste ground. It has some culinary uses and a variety of medicinal applications.

Also known as "stinging nettle," the scientific name of the common nettle comes from the Latin word *urere*, meaning "to burn." This tough perennial, with its stinging hairs, is well known as a fast-growing weed throughout temperate parts of Europe and Asia. It seems to spring up wherever people settle, especially around waste sites, as it enjoys soil that is rich in nitrogen.

There is much more to this plant than being a troublesome weed, however, and it has a long history of varied use, both culinary and medicinal. Nettles can be used in soups—its most familiar application—or prepared rather like spinach. This astringent plant is also an ideal ingredient in bath, facial, and hair preparations. It has detoxifying, diuretic and tonic properties that can be used to boost the circulation, lower blood pressure, and control bleeding, as well as ease rheumatism and urinary disorders.

Mysterious Origins

Nettle crops up throughout history. It has been used to make paper, rope, and cloth. Bronze Age peoples used nettle fiber for cloth, as did the Scots during the 1600s—the poet Campbell wrote: "I have eaten nettles, I have slept in nettle sheets, and I have dined off a nettle tablecloth." During World War I, the Germans made uniforms from nettle fiber when short of cotton. Various countries also used it as a green-yellow dye. Today, nettles are grown commercially for chlorophyll, to color medicines and food.

Coping with Stings

The whole plant is covered with fine hairs, and the base of each hollow hair contains a stinging acid. When the sharp tip of a hair pierces the skin, the acid is released. The cooling juice of various leaves—notably dock, but also, ironically, the juice of the nettle leaf itself—will bring relief. This stinging effect is destroyed by heating or wilting.

USES

PARTS USED:
Leaves, whole plant.

PROPERTIES:
Astringent, diuretic, tonic herb; clears toxins; controls bleeding; reduces blood pressure and blood sugar levels.

USES OF THE HERB:
Culinary
Ignore recommendations to use as a salad leaf—the leaves are highly irritating when raw. Cook young shoots and leaves like spinach.

Medicinal
Infusions can be applied externally to help skin problems such as eczema, scalp conditions, bites, burns, and arthritis. Taken internally for arthritis, rheumatism, anemia, hemorrhoids, skin problems, and heavy menstruation.

Cosmetic
Effective as a skin and hair treatment.

Household
Can be used as a green-yellow dye.

CAUTION
Raw leaves are an irritant.

Stem
The stem is square and covered with hairs.

Leaf
Broadly heart-shaped, pointed, and toothed leaves are covered with fine, stinging hairs.

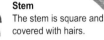

Flower
Male and female flowers—drooping spikes of small green blooms—are usually borne on separate plants from July to October.

Spicy Nut
Nutmeg spice comes from the kernels or "nuts," dried thoroughly and sold whole, to be grated as desired. It is also available as a finely ground powder, although this is a poor substitute for freshly ground nutmeg.

Leaf
Long, elliptical leaves are a glossy dark green on the upper sides, and aromatic.

Fruit
Fleshy, apricot-like fruit bursts open when ripe to reveal the kernel, encased in the scarlet mace.

Nutmeg Spice
The scarlet mace is dried, turning orange, and used as a culinary flavoring. The nutmeg contains a volatile oil, which provides its balsamic aroma and flavor.

NUTMEG

Once used mainly for its medicinal qualities, nutmeg is now popular as a culinary flavoring in both sweet and savory dishes.

The spice known as nutmeg is made from the dried seed of a fragrant evergreen tree which is native to tropical islands in Southeast Asia. The aril, a red casing around this seed, is also dried and used to produce another spice—mace.

The essential oil of the nutmeg seed gives the powdered or grated spice an exotic and balsamic nature that lends itself to a host of culinary uses. It is especially suitable for cakes, breads, sweet sauces, desserts, and milky drinks—it is used as a topping for eggnog. It is excellent in fruit recipes; with vegetables such as cabbage, pumpkin, mashed potatoes, and spinach; in cheese dishes; and with meat. Oily extracts ("nutmeg butter") are used commercially in products such as soaps.

Nutmeg's early history mainly concerns its therapeutic uses—this was one of the remedies used by the physicians of ancient China. It is a stimulating substance that contains an hallucinogen. In moderate amounts, the spice improves digestion and appetite, aids stomach upsets and diarrhea, eases insomnia, and, applied externally, may relieve pains such as rheumatism. Large doses however, can have the opposite effect, producing vomiting, headaches, and delirium.

Arab Spice
The Arabs probably brought this spice to European shores around the first century AD. During the 1500s, Portugal gained control of certain Indonesian spice islands and, with them, the nutmeg trade, which was later commercialized by the Dutch. The spice continued to be known as a stimulant and tonic as well as a talisman against ill fortune.

Today, the spice is used mainly in cooking, and trees are cultivated in tropical areas—mainly Indonesia, Sri Lanka, and the West Indies.

USES

PARTS USED:
Seeds, oil.

PROPERTIES:
Bitter, astringent, spicy herb; anti-inflammatory.

USES OF THE HERB:
Culinary
Add to, or sprinkle onto, creamy or milky desserts and drinks; use in cakes and breads, sweet or savory sauces, with vegetables (such as cabbage, mashed potatoes and spinach) and with various meats.

Medicinal
This stimulant boosts the appetite and digestion and, applied externally, can ease rheumatic pain.

Cosmetic
Added to exotic perfumes and soaps.

Household
Used in fragrant candles.

CAUTION
Large doses of this hallucinogen can cause adverse side effects.

OREGANO

This herb, with its culinary and medicinal properties, has a history dating back to the ancient Egyptians. It is one of the few herbs that retains its flavor and aroma when dried.

There are about twenty species of *Origanum*. Among these many species are the herbs commonly known as "oregano" and "marjoram." Hybrids between cultivated species abound, which often makes precise identification difficult. Confusingly, true oregano (*Origanum vulgare*) is also known as wild marjoram, while the classic marjoram herb is either sweet marjoram (*O. majorana*) or pot marjoram (*O. onites*). Commercial dried oregano (used for culinary purposes) is produced from several different species.

Aromatic Properties
Oregano is well known for its aromatic properties—in summer, it covers hillsides across Europe and central Asia and fills the air with its sweet, distinctive scent. This fragrance is preserved by drying, and the herb is used to great effect in products such as scented sachets and potpourri.

Plant of the Ancients
Oregano has been famed for its wide-ranging medicinal properties since the days of ancient Egypt. The warming, slightly antiseptic nature of oregano gives it an excellent reputation for calming fevers, nervous headaches, and irritability, and helping the digestive system.

Garden Favorite
Fragrant and easy to cultivate, oregano looks attractive wherever it grows, with its pink-purple flowers dotted against dark green leaves. Other variations have entirely golden or gold-dipped leaves, and the flowers can be white in color. Low-growing, golden varieties of oregano make attractive aromatic edging plants. However, they are a favorite of insects too, so think about where you plant this herb if bees bother you.

Leaf
The whole plant, including leaves, stems, and flowers, can be dried for use in cooking, and for medicinal and cosmetic purposes.

USES

PARTS USED:
Leaves, flowers, and stems.

PROPERTIES:
Aromatic, antiseptic

USES OF THE HERB:
Culinary
Mainly used in dried form, oregano provides a strong flavoring that complements ingredients such as chilli, garlic, tomato, and onion. Oregano oil is used in many commercially branded foods and sauces.

Medicinal
Tea made from the leaves and flowers is good for coughs, colds and flu, indigestion, and period pain. Steam inhalation is used for bronchitis and asthma. Compresses can be applied for arthritis and muscular pain. Oil is used in aromatherapy to treat these conditions.

Cosmetic
Oil is used in toiletries and perfumes.

Decorative
Golden marjoram is a popular garden plant for its colored leaves, which fade as flowering begins and scorch in sunlight. Dry leaves and flowers for potpourri.

CAUTION
Avoid during pregnancy. May irritate the skin if used externally.

Dried Oregano
The dried, crushed leaves are used as a flavoring ingredient in many dishes, especially pizza.

Seeds
Used to propagate the plant in spring or autumn.

Culinary Delights
Whether infused as tea, added to salads, or sprinkled over pizza, the herb has an unmistakable flavor. The name comes from the Greek *origanon*, meaning "bitter herb."

PARSLEY

Probably the most widely used of all culinary herbs, fresh parsley provides flavor to cooked and uncooked food, and also makes an attractive garnish. It is suitable for planting in the garden as well as in containers.

Parsley was originally native to southern Europe, but it is now grown throughout the world. Brought to Britain by the Romans, it gained huge popularity as a culinary herb. We now know its dark green curly leaves contain vitamins A and C and plenty of minerals and iron.

Growing Parsley

Three main types of parsley can easily be grown in the garden. The first is the "curled" or "garden" parsley that makes a wonderful garnish for soups and salads. It is also a common ingredient of bouquet garni. Other varieties include Italian or French parsley, which has flatter leaves and a stronger flavor. An infusion of this herb is said to revive the appetite. The third type—the large turnip-root or Hamburg parsley—is less widely grown. It is used either as a root vegetable or as a tea to aid rheumatism.

Parsley is a biennial but is best grown on an annual basis. It has tiny flowers in the second year, but this means that it is past its best and should be discarded. By sowing at regular intervals, you should be able to pick parsley all year round—especially if you protect it from frost with a cloche. It can be transplanted or sown on site. The seed can be slow to germinate but usually succeeds if the ground is warm and moist. Soaking in lukewarm water for two hours before sowing may speed germination.

Medicinal Aid

Parsley tea has a very beneficial effect on the urinary system and is an excellent treatment for kidney and bladder complaints. Chew on parsley to sweeten the breath and, in particular, to counter the smell of garlic.

Leaf
Curly, with a saw-toothed edge. Bright green and fresh-tasting, the leaves are an important source of vitamins and minerals.

Stem
Strong, edible stems have more flavor than the leaves.

Seeds
Small, grayish-brown seeds can be toxic if taken in excess.

Dried Parsley Leaves
Parsley leaves retain their flavor well when dried but are best added late in the cooking process.

USES

PARTS USED:
Leaves and stems; the root of Hamburg parsley is also used.

PROPERTIES:
Contains vitamins, minerals, and iron; diuretic.

USES OF THE HERB:
Culinary
Add raw parsley to salads. Finely chop and sprinkle in sandwiches, egg dishes, soups, fish, and potatoes. It is an ingredient of many classic sauces.

Medicinal
Make an infusion of parsley leaves to aid digestion. It has a diuretic action and can be taken by those suffering from fluid retention and for helping with arthritis and osteoarthritis. Take one teaspoon of leaves to a cup of boiling water three times daily.

CAUTION
Parsley should not be taken in medicinal doses by pregnant women or those with stomach ulcers. A poisonous weed, *Aethusa cynapium* (known as "fool's parsley") resembles flat-leaved Italian parsley, so do not pick this plant in the wild.

ROSEMARY

A versatile herb, with many culinary and medicinal applications. It grows readily in warm, dry conditions, is evergreen, and produces flowers in the early spring.

This distinctive herb has a wonderful and instantly identifiable aroma that has made it popular in cooking and medicine for many centuries. Today, rosemary is best known as a culinary herb. It is generally used to flavor roast meats and to add flavor and aroma to herb oils and vinegars. Rosemary grows into a sizable bush, covered with needlelike leaves that, when crushed, release the volatile oil and scent. But it is also a valuable garden plant. It has many varieties, with flowers varying in color from white, through pink, to blue. It is also fast growing, while its height and density make it suitable for use as a garden hedge. Four hundred years ago, rosemary was used for just this purpose, often trimmed into fanciful shapes. It was also used in weddings, to deck the church and make bridal wreaths.

Folk Remedies
Rosemary's history is rich in folklore going back to biblical times. One tale has it as the bush that shielded the Virgin Mary as she fled to Egypt. Its flowers were originally white but turned blue to match the color of her cloak.

Most of the stories concern rosemary's aromatic properties. Its scent was believed to ward off disease and was often used to purify the air in sick chambers. It was carried during plagues, to be sniffed while passing through areas of possible infection. In ancient times, scholars wore rosemary garlands to strengthen the memory. Thus the plant came to be associated with fidelity.

USES

PARTS USED:
Leaves and stems.

PROPERTIES:
Stimulating and aromatic, this herb contains a volatile oil used for a variety of medicinal treatments and culinary applications.

USES OF THE HERB:
Culinary
Use fresh or dried leaves or sprigs of the herb to flavor meat while roasting. Use fresh sprigs to flavor herb oils and vinegars, and use fresh leaves sparingly in herb butters. Fresh rosemary is delicious in salads. Burn branches on a barbecue to flavor meat.

Medicinal
Rosemary is a very good all-around tonic. It stimulates circulation and increases blood supply, and has

been used as a remedy for hardening of the arteries. Take as an infusion three times daily. Rosemary can also lift mild depression and is good for treating headaches and migraines.**

Cosmetic
Use the essential oil in *eau de cologne*. Use fresh or dried leaves in a facial steam to stimulate circulation. Infuse leaves as a rinse for dark hair.

CAUTION
Not recommended for epileptics. Avoid during pregnancy and while breastfeeding. Don't take rosemary to excess at any time.

Leaf
Tough, needlelike leaves release their aromatic oil when crushed.

Stem
Tough and woody by the second year. Branches can be burnt to release aromatic smoke, but strip away all leaves to discourage flaring.

Flavoring
Rosemary sprigs can be steeped in vinegar or olive oil to provide a distinctive flavor.

Dried Leaf
A basic of many flavorings, dried leaves retain their flavor well in storage.

SAFFRON CROCUS

Saffron is probably the most labor-intensive herb to harvest. This is what makes it precious, and is also why cheaper substitutes are sometimes passed off as the real thing.

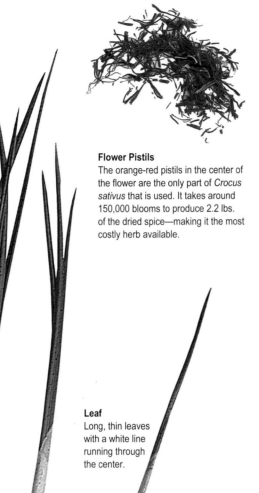

Flower Pistils
The orange-red pistils in the center of the flower are the only part of *Crocus sativus* that is used. It takes around 150,000 blooms to produce 2.2 lbs. of the dried spice—making it the most costly herb available.

Leaf
Long, thin leaves with a white line running through the center.

Stem
Short, encased in sheaths. Underground, the globular stem-base forms a flattened corm.

Saffron is the world's most exclusive and costly herb from a weight perspective—it takes 150,000 flowers to produce 2.2 pounds of the famous yellow-staining saffron spice. The only part of the herb used is the pistil—the orange-red stigma and styles in the center of the bloom. The pistil is removed by hand, dried, and sold whole or as a powder that dissolves and turns bright yellow in water.

Long-prized Spice
Prized since ancient times, saffron features in the traditional dishes of several nations, such as Spanish paella and zarzuela (fish stew), French bouillabaisse, Italian risotto Milanese, and a wide variety of Indian and other Eastern sauces. It is also used in cakes. Fortunately, given its cost, only a minute amount is needed to produce its distinctive color and flavor. Saffron also has various therapeutic properties and is known in traditional Chinese medicine as *fan hong hua*, prescribed for depression and certain menstrual problems. It aids digestion, stimulates perspiration, and reduces high blood pressure. Saffron tea is said to lift the spirits and calm the nerves.

Colorful History
The name "saffron" is derived from the Arabic *za'fân*, meaning "yellow," and the herb was being used as a culinary spice as far back as the tenth century BC. The Greeks knew it as *krokos,* and the Romans as *karkom*, and it was mentioned in the Bible in the Song of Solomon. From Persia and India, the herb was brought to China during the Yuan Dynasty (1279–1368). It arrived in Europe during the Crusades and was a popular dye for textiles, hair, and nails. Greedy traders adulterated saffron with fake dyed fibers from other sources.

Many places are famous for saffron cultivation—including Saffron Walden, in England, which takes its name from the spice—but today the best is grown in Kashmir and Spain.

USES

PARTS USED:
Flower pistils.

PROPERTIES:
Bittersweet, pungent; aids digestion, increases perspiration, reduces high blood pressure, and stimulates circulation and menstruation.

USES OF THE HERB:
Medicinal
Used in Chinese medicine for depression and menstrual dysfunction. Aids digestion, eases flatulence, stimulates perspiration, and reduces high blood pressure.

Culinary
Long used in Eastern dishes, also in French bouillabaisse, Spanish paella and zarzuela (fish stew), Italian risotto Milanese, and cakes.

Cosmetic
Formerly used to dye hair and nails.

Household
Once used to scent seats and floors; cushions stuffed with leaves.

CAUTION
Do not confuse with poisonous meadow saffron (*Colchicum autumnale*).

SAGE

This low-growing aromatic herb has a reputation for its healing properties as well as its culinary value. Taller and more colorful varieties are also grown as ornamentals.

Sage is among the most versatile kitchen herbs—but as it has a strong flavor, it is best used on its own rather than together with other herbs. It combines well with rich and fatty foods, breaking them down as an aid to digestion. Sage is often used with meats such as pork, duck, and sausage, and is a classic companion to liver. Sage contains powerful medicinal ingredients and has been credited throughout history with promoting a long life and restoring memory in the elderly.

Sacred Herb

Sage's Latin name *Salvia* comes from a word meaning "to cure" or "save." The Romans gathered it with great ceremony, treating it as sacred. Infusions of the leaves were used to treat fevers and to stimulate the nervous system. It was supposed to stem bleeding, and the juice was used to treat snake bites.

The plant originates from the Mediterranean but happily survives colder climates. Grown in the garden, its soft gray-green leaves make an ideal contrast to darker, spiky herbs such as rosemary while giving off a delightful and distinctive aroma. The leaves are evergreen. Sage flowers are small and usually mauve in color, although white and pink forms are found. Bees love the blooms, and in hot climates such as Greece, where the plants flower prolifically, sage honey is much sought after and commands high prices.

There are over half a dozen varieties, with leaves ranging in color from gold to purple, some of which are variegated. Among the varieties, purple sage (*Salvia officinalis* "Purpurascens" group) shares the culinary properties of common sage but has even more outstanding medicinal qualities.

Leaf
Gray-green, thick, and downy with heavily veined underside. Can be dried for cooking, medicinal, and cosmetic purposes.

Stem
Square and covered with fine hairs. The stems become woody by the second year.

Seeds
Tiny, dark brown, and egg-shaped.

USES

PARTS USED:
Leaves, seeds.

PROPERTIES:
Aromatic, healing.

USES OF THE HERB:
Culinary
Use fresh or dried leaves to make sage and onion stuffing, and to flavor duck, pork, liver, or sausage meat. Blend the chopped herb into cheese or butter and use in cream sauces. Use to flavor oils and vinegars. Eat purple sage with pork, veal, and game.

Medicinal
Purple sage can be drunk as an infusion at the first sign of any respiratory infections. It soothes inflammations of the mouth and throat, and is an effective gargle. Pour boiling water onto one to two teaspoons of the dried leaves and leave to infuse for ten minutes.

Household
Burn dried leaves or boil in water to neutralize cooking or animal odors in a room. Dried sage in potpourri or sachets among clothes discourages insects.

CAUTION
Although small amounts are quite safe when cooking, pregnant and breastfeeding women should not take therapeutic doses. Sage contains thujone, which can trigger fits in epileptics.

Leaf
Crown of long, lance-shaped, blue-
or yellow-tinged leaves, arranged
in large, attractive fans. Leafstalks
often have sharp spines.

SAW PALMETTO

Popular as a garden ornamental, this tropical-looking palm is hardy, drought resistant, and trouble-free. Its fruits are the source of a remedy used for a variety of conditions.

Named after the sharp spines often found along its leafstalks, this tough, low-growing evergreen palm is native to the coastal fringe of the southeastern United States. It goes by a host of other names, including "sabal."

Body-builder
The plant is famed for its fleshy fruits—edible but rather unpleasant tasting—and herbal remedies made from fruit extracts are now widely available. Both sedative and tonic, this warming herb helps to build a strong constitution, keeping the all-important mucous membranes in good condition and so keeping the reproductive, respiratory, and digestive systems healthy. It is said to act on the body's hormonal system in a way that is as yet not understood, and currently its best known use is for prostate-related problems, loss of libido, and impotence. Remedies are also said to be diuretic, expectorant, astringent, and antiseptic, and aid conditions such as cystitis, uterine inflammation, bronchial infections, and colds.

Native Food
The palm's scientific name comes from the nineteenth-century American botanist Sereno Watson, who was the first to draw up detailed descriptions of a large number of North American plants. In the 1700s, European settlers found Native Americans in the southeast using the seeds and fruit for food, as a general tonic, and as a treatment for impotence, testicular problems, enlarged prostate, poor lactation, female infertility, painful menstruation, tender or underdeveloped breasts, and low libido. The settlers were struck by how healthy people became when eating large amounts of the fruit.

Natural Resistance
Saw palmetto is the only species in its genus. Now an increasingly popular ornamental—raised from seeds at specialist nurseries since it does not transplant well from the wild—it is valued for the large fans formed by its long, pointed leaves. It is also naturally resistant to insect attack and drought.

USES

PARTS USED:
Fruits.

PROPERTIES:
Astringent, diuretic, expectorant, sedative, and warming; tonic effect; affects the endocrine system, acts as a urinary antiseptic; vanilla-like aroma; reputedly an aphrodisiac.

USES OF THE HERB:
Medicinal
Remedies made from fruits are known principally for their action on prostate gland and for libido; also maintain healthy tissues and mucous membranes in all the main systems of the body. Taken for poor general health, cystitis, uterine inflammation, poor lactation, tender breasts during menstruation and breastfeeding, catarrh, colds, asthma.

Seed
Hard and brown.

SELF-HEAL

As its name indicates, this plant is essentially a medicinal one. It has a long tradition as a cure for a variety of ailments and also has antiseptic properties. It can be cultivated as part of a wildflower bed.

Also known popularly as "heal-all," this aromatic and attractive plant has long been valued for its medicinal properties. It was once used to treat quinsy—inflammations of the throat or tonsils—and the genus name is a variant of *brunella*, which comes from a German word for this condition.

Healing Properties

In European folk medicine, this astringent and bitter plant is known for its healing abilities—especially with regard to minor wounds and problems such as cuts, burns, bruising, hemorrhoids, and mouth or throat infections—since extracts from the whole plant appear to have a natural antiseptic action. Preparations have also been taken to relieve heavy menstruation and hemorrhaging. Self-heal is a diuretic that stimulates the liver, and practitioners of traditional Chinese medicine have recommended flower extracts for two thousand years for problems linked with that organ, as well as for reducing high blood pressure, headaches, mumps, mastitis, and certain eye infections. It is also said to lower fever and acts as a revitalizing tonic for the body in aiding the breakdown and expulsion of potentially toxic waste products.

Attractive Wildflower

With its pleasant aroma and dense spikes of purple flowers, lasting through the summer and on into autumn, this hardy plant makes an attractive addition to wildflower displays, though it is not really showy enough to be a centerpiece species in the garden. Height varies from an inch to twenty inches, depending on conditions (it will grow taller in shady spots), but it is commonly a low-grower, making it ideal for rockeries, edging, and as ground cover.

Self-heal can start to spread rather rapidly, so it is a good choice for planters and contained spaces—beware it creeping into lawns—but is not too difficult to bring under control. Other varieties are available with pale mauve, pink, or white flowers.

Leaf
Oval, glossy leaves turn from green to yellow or red in autumn.

Flower
Spikes of dark purple blooms last into autumn.

Stem
Squared stem; main stem rough, sometimes grooved. Puts out branches freely.

Seed
Of no medicinal use.

USES

PARTS USED:
Whole plant, flowers.

PROPERTIES:
Astringent, diuretic, antibacterial, slightly bitter, saline herb; promotes healing, stimulates the liver and gallbladder, lowers fever and blood pressure.

USES OF THE HERB:
Medicinal
Used externally, a self-heal compress or poultice will aid the healing of small wounds, burns, bruises, hemorrhoids, and so on, while a mouthwash will ease throat and mouth infections. Taken internally, it may help to reduce heavy menstruation, aid internal ulcers, and provide a tonic for the liver—the Chinese use it for complaints associated with weakness of the liver. Also eases fever, mumps, headaches, mastitis, eye infections, and high blood pressure.

Leaf
Bright green, dock-like
leaves have a distinct
lemony scent.

Stem
Ridged stem is tinged
with red.

SORREL

The ancient Romans used sorrel to cure scurvy—but
nowadays it is mainly used for its tangy flavor, added to
salads and soups, or cooked with other leafy vegetables.

This hardy perennial belongs to a large genus of about two hundred
plants and is found across northern temperate areas. The use of
common sorrel dates back many centuries, to the days of the Roman
Empire, when it is said that soldiers took a particular variety to cure
themselves of scurvy. As a plant, common sorrel falls somewhere
between an herb and a vegetable and is grown for its dock-like leaves,
which add a very tangy flavor to soups, sauces, and salads. This herb
should be used in small quantities since it has an acidic flavor.

Sorrel is less well known as a medicinal plant, but it does have various
therapeutic uses, thanks to its astringent, cooling, and diuretic effects.
Tea made from the leaves can be used to lower fevers and treat liver
and kidney problems, while leaf poultices ease certain skin complaints.
However, many *Rumex* varieties contain oxalates, which are highly
acidic and possibly poisonous if taken in large amounts. The concentrated juice of *Rumex acetosa* is used in preparations designed to
bleach and remove difficult stains such as rust and mold.

Close Relations
Closely related is *Rumex scutatus*, French sorrel, which has a slightly
milder flavor than common sorrel. Dock species, such as *Rumex
crispus*, are also included in this genus but are generally less palatable
than sorrel. Common sorrel has a distinctive appearance. As well
as dock-like leaves, it produces spikes of rust-colored flowers in
summer and tiny fruits shortly afterward. It has deep roots and, once
established, can spread like a weed. For this reason, it is a good idea
to grow it as an annual—especially since the young leaves have a less
astringent flavor than those on more mature perennial specimens.

Plants should be propagated by sowing seeds during spring and by
dividing plants in spring or autumn. Leaves should be picked when
young, and used fresh.

USES

PARTS USED:
Leaves.

PROPERTIES:
**Cooling, astringent, acidic herb;
diuretic effects.**

USES OF THE HERB:
Culinary
**Add fresh leaves to salads, soups,
and sauces and some egg dishes.
Chopped or puréed leaves may
be mixed in with soft cheese or
mayonnaise.**

Medicinal
**Not commonly used medicinally,
but its diuretic effects can help with
certain kidney and liver complaints,
while, applied externally, its cooling**

**properties may ease skin problems
such as boils and acne.**

Household
**Used in stain removers and may
be used as a green and yellow
vegetable dye.**

Decorative
**The seed heads are attractive if
included in arrangements and
wreaths.**

CAUTION
**May be detrimental to health if
consumed in large quantities.**

Seeds
Small, brown seeds are
pointed in shape.

ST JOHN'S WORT

This flowering perennial is part of folklore and has a long history as a healing plant. Scientific research substantiates its medicinal properties and is finding more and more ways of using it.

This cheery, golden-flowered perennial is native to the hedgerows and woodlands of Europe and temperate Asia. Prized as a healing herb since ancient times, it contains a powerful substance called "hypericin," now being investigated by scientists looking for a cure for AIDS. Hypericin is also a well-established antidepressant, although it is not suitable for those suffering from chronic depression.

Healing Qualities
St John's Wort sometimes causes dermatitis, especially on skin exposed to direct sunlight, and the raw plant can be harmful if eaten. But it has a host of healing qualities—it acts as a local antiseptic and painkiller, soothes jittery nerves, speeds natural healing, and reduces inflammation. It is good for toothache, shooting pains, and hemorrhoids. Taken internally, this herb can relieve shingles, sciatica, premenstrual tension, and menopausal problems, as well as fibrosis.

External Use
Used externally, St John's Wort relieves skin sores, minor burns, bruises, cramps, sprains, and other injuries involving damage to the nerves, such as tennis elbow. The plant also features in various guises in homeopathic and traditional Indian ayurvedic remedies.

Magical Properties
Hypericin, a bright red pigment, leaks from the crushed flowers of this herb rather like blood—one reason for the ancient belief in its magical properties. Hypericin probably derives from the Greek *hyper*, meaning "above," and *eikon*, "picture," because the flowers were hung above religious icons to ward off evil on St John's Day (June 24). The common name comes from John the Baptist, beheaded at the request of Salome, King Herod's stepdaughter. The red pigment from the crushed flowers is said to symbolize his blood. Today the whole plant is usually harvested just as it is flowering and used fresh or dried. In Australia it is a serious weed and is subject to statutory controls.

USES

PARTS USED:
Whole plant.

PROPERTIES:
Astringent, bitter, cooling herb; reduces inflammation, promotes healing, and calms nerves; local antiseptic and painkiller.

USES OF THE HERB:
Medicinal
Tackles inflammation, nerve pain, and injury. Promotes healing. Internally for bed-wetting in children, anxiety, premenstrual syndrome, menopausal problems, sciatica, fibrosis, and shingles. Good for toothache, shooting pains, neuralgia, concussion, nausea, hemorrhoids. Externally for burns, bruises, **sprains, cramp, tennis elbow, and any kind of nerve damage. Used in homeopathy and ayurvedic medicine.**

CAUTION
Should not be given to patients with chronic depression. Can be harmful if eaten raw. May cause dermatitis, especially in direct sunlight. May reduce effectiveness of the contraceptive pill.

Flower
Clusters of golden, five-petaled flowers, around ¾ in. across, from June to September.

Leaf
Opposite, ovate to linear leaves with translucent dots.

Antidepressant
St John's Wort contains a potent chemical called hypericin, recently recognized as an antidepressant, which leaks from the crushed flowers as a red pigment. Hypericin has also been subject to scientific research as a possible cure for AIDS.

Stem
Round, erect, hairless stem.

SUNFLOWER

Apart from the sheer loveliness of the brightly colored blooms, which are popular with florists, sunflower plants also provide a range of culinary and medicinal products.

Flower
Distinctive, sunlike blooms have vivid yellow ray florets encircling a central disc of purple-brown tube florets.

In a history spanning many centuries, it is said that the Aztecs crowned their sun priestesses with these giant, daisy-like flowers, and the scientific name is actually derived from the Greek word *helios*, meaning "sun." Sunflowers have a wide range of uses, and the entire plant can be used. They make an eye-catching display when grown against a sunny wall or fence, and the seeds are delicious raw or toasted and in salads, breads, and all kinds of other dishes. Sprouting sunflower seeds are another tasty and healthy addition to salad dishes. Even the flower buds of this plant can be eaten raw in salads or steamed as a vegetable.

Life Enhancing
The polyunsaturated oil pressed from the seeds is a healthy choice for cooking and salad dressings and is also used in margarine. Sunflower remedies can be taken to combat complaints as diverse as rheumatism and malaria. Also, they have been grown to help reclaim land in marshy expanses of Holland because of their unusual capacity for absorbing water.

Sunflowers were grown by Native American peoples for several thousand years before being brought to Spain in the 1500s. Germany and Russia led the way in commercial cultivation during the 1700s and, since then, the plants have been a very important commercial crop because of their oil-rich seeds. There are seventy to eighty annuals and perennials within the *Helianthus* genus. All of them are tall, although smaller varieties, such as the dwarf cultivar *H. annuus* "Teddy Bear," have been developed.

Garden Giant
The classic sunflower stands at a towering ten feet, with massive single blooms, produced between August and October. Sunflowers like a sunny position in well-drained soil, and, although hardy, the seeds may not ripen if the weather turns damp and chilly in the fall.

Stem
Thick, upright stem is hairy and light green in color.

Sunflower Oil
Extracted from the seeds, sunflower oil is a high-quality polyunsaturated product.

Seeds
Edible seeds are flat, oval and usually gray striped with white; the kernels are high in nutrients.

USES

PARTS USED:
Seeds, stems, leaves, and flowers

PROPERTIES:
Polyunsaturated oil extracted from plant valuable for lowering cholesterol levels.

USES OF THE HERB:
Culinary
Sunflower seed oil is used for general cooking and salad dressings, while the seeds and kernels can be eaten raw or toasted. Add sprouted seeds to salads and sandwiches. Seeds are also ground into flour for baking.

Medicinal
Valuable for lowering blood cholesterol levels—so using the oil as part of a healthy eating program is recommended. Remedies can help ease malaria, bronchitis, and tuberculosis. The oil is also a good base for aromatherapy and massage oils used to treat muscular aches and pains.

Decorative
Sunflower seed heads make an attractive addition to floral arrangements.

TARRAGON

Well known as a culinary herb, this plant is also used medicinally. The leaves contain vitamin A, minerals, and trace elements. It is easily cultivated and is at its best used fresh.

The unique flavor of this aromatic and versatile herb has long made it popular among chefs, and it is a classic element of French cuisine. It is one of the more important ingredients of *fines herbes* and a number of sauces. The leaves contain vitamin A, niacin, calcium, and iron. The *Artemisia* genus, of which tarragon is a member, includes some very bitter herbs indeed. Among these is wormwood, which is used to treat worms and also to stimulate the digestive system. Tarragon is the only herb in the genus that is not too bitter to be used in cooking, and it can be used quite generously.

The Latin name for tarragon is *dracunculus*, meaning "little dragon," which may refer to its supposed ability to cure poisonous bites. Originally from central Asia, it is likely that tarragon was introduced to Europe during the Moorish occupation of southern Spain at the end of the Middle Ages.

Growing Tarragon
Tarragon is a creeping perennial, and its narrow, aromatic leaves contrast well with other foliage in the herb garden. It can also be grown outdoors in large pots and moved to a cold frame in autumn to give protection. Small green flowers appear in early to mid summer and should be pinched out to encourage leafy growth. In colder areas the plant may not flower at all.

Two kinds of tarragon are commonly cultivated—French tarragon (*dracunculus*) and Russian tarragon (*dracunculoides*). The French is infinitely superior to the Russian, which is not as highly flavored. Tarragon sold as seed is almost always Russian tarragon. When buying plants, note that Russian tarragon has thinner, paler leaves than its French counterpart.

Dried Leaf
Contains far less flavor than the fresh leaf and may lose this with age.

Flavored Vinegar
A sprig of fresh tarragon can be used to flavor vinegar for use in salad dressings and when making mayonnaise.

Stem
Round and branching, can become brown and woody near the base of the plant.

Root
Dense and fine. Has been used to cure toothache.

USES

PARTS USED:
Leaves.

PROPERTIES:
Aromatic, diuretic.

USES OF THE HERB:
Culinary
Use the leaves with chicken and egg dishes, soups, stuffings, and sauces for fish. A classic ingredient of *fines herbes* (with chervil and parsley), tarragon vinegar, herb butter, and sauce béarnaise and hollandaise. Good with many cream sauces. Very compatible with asparagus. Use to season strong-flavored fish, liver, and roast duck.

Medicinal
Medicinal uses are limited, although it is good for digestion and can help delayed menstruation. Destroys intestinal worms and acts as a diuretic.

CAUTION
Do not take in medicinal quantity during pregnancy, but culinary use is no problem.

Culinary Favorite
This herb is easily grown in well-drained soil in full sun. It is also suitable for a container and combines well with other culinary herbs.

Seeds
Shiny-brown, tiny, and spherical.

Leaf
Aromatic and pointed, mid green, with rolled edges and fine hairs underneath.

Dried Leaf
Used to flavor sauces and stocks. Retains strong flavor.

Root
Thyme forms a fine, dense mat of thin brown roots.

THYME

Every part of this herb is used—the leaves, fresh or dried, are used in the kitchen and infusions, and extracts from the rest of the plant have medicinal uses.

Common thyme is a small, aromatic herb with a bushy habit. It is a member of a large genus with a range of uses. The leaves of different varieties may be green, gray, golden, or variegated, and the flowers can be lilac, white, or one of many shades of pink. There are several other useful varieties, including lemon thyme (*Thymus citriodorus*). Common thyme (*T. vulgaris*) has wide-ranging culinary properties and a reputation for aiding the digestion of rich foods. It is used to flavor stocks, stuffings, and soups, and blends well in sauces for poultry, fish, and pork. Thyme has a powerful antibacterial effect, stimulating the immune system. It can be used to medicate surgical dressings (since it does not irritate the skin), to drive away insects, and as an inhalation to ease breathing problems. An extract, thymol, is used in many toothpastes and mouthwashes, and the essential oil is used for aches, pains, and skin disorders.

Heaven Scent
Thyme grows wild around the Mediterranean, where its fragrance scents the hillsides. The Greeks called it *thymus*, which means "courage." They used it for massage oil, and Roman soldiers are reputed to have bathed in thyme water before battle. Its antiseptic and preservative qualities were recognized by the ancient Egyptians, who used it in embalming fluid and burnt it to fumigate rooms. Thyme grows well in colder climates, provided the soil is well drained. It makes a good ground cover in borders or rock gardens, and the flowers attract bees.

USES

PARTS USED:
Whole plant, leaves, flowering tops, oil.

PROPERTIES:
Aromatic, astringent, expectorant, antiseptic, and antifungal.

USES OF THE HERB:
Culinary
Dry the leaf, chop finely, and use to make bouquet garni with parsley and bay. Use the fresh leaf to flavor stuffings, stocks, and soups, and to cook chicken, fish, and shellfish. Use sprigs of the fresh herb in cooking oils and vinegars.

Medicinal
An infusion of thyme leaves will aid digestion. Combine with honey for troublesome coughs and sore throats and deep-seated chest infections. It can also help to clear asthma, catarrh, laryngitis, and bronchitis but should not be taken for longer than three weeks at a time.

Cosmetic
Use fresh or dried herbs in facial steams to cleanse the skin.

Decorative
Use flowering sprigs in summer flower arrangements.

Household
Use essential oil mixed with alcohol to spray on paper and pressed flower specimens as a mold inhibitor. Make up a decoction to use as a mild disinfectant.

CAUTION
Avoid therapeutic doses during pregnancy.

TURMERIC

Widely used as a coloring and flavoring ingredient in food, turmeric also has various properties put to medicinal use.

This tropical perennial and Indian native produces one of the best-known Asian spices—used in all kinds of dishes and with a long history of medical use. For both culinary and medicinal use, the large, tapering rhizomes are the significant part of the plant. These are dried and ground into a powder, often used commercially in mass-market curry powders. Turmeric powder has a slightly acrid aroma; a bitter, warming taste; and a very vivid yellow color—this is the traditional dye used to color the robes of Buddhist monks, and it is also used to color a wide variety of savory foods.

As a therapeutic agent, this mildly aromatic and stimulating spice is thought to have an anti-inflammatory effect and to improve the healthy functioning of the body's major systems. Turmeric also has a certain antibiotic effect and can be used to treat minor wounds and sores.

Chinese Tradition
Practitioners of traditional Chinese medicine were recommending the use of turmeric as long ago as the fifth century. According to their system, turmeric is a substance that helps to balance the body's energy. It has also long been a feature of medical treatments in various other parts of Asia—and was once used to treat jaundice. Today, research seems to indicate that this spice protects and improves the health of the liver. Research is also investigating its possible use as an anti-inflammatory agent. It is also used to color various medicines.

Valuable Rhizomes
The tapering rhizomes are light brown on the outside and bright yellow-orange on the inside. The rhizomes are collected when dormant and then either steamed or boiled, and dried carefully before being ground into turmeric powder for use in decoctions, pills, and powders.

Cultivation
The turmeric plant, a tender perennial, needs ample warmth and humidity, with minimum temperatures of around 60ºF if it is to thrive. It is unsuitable for outdoor cultivation in temperate regions, although, given the right conditions, it can be grown under cover in a greenhouse or conservatory.

USES

PARTS USED:
Rhizomes.

PROPERTIES:
Aromatic, astringent, bitter and pungent; anti-inflammatory, anti-bacterial, and stimulant.

USES OF THE HERB:
Culinary
Use to color and flavor all kinds of curry dishes, vegetable soups, and rice.

Medicinal
Turmeric stimulates the systems of the body, including the digestion and functioning of the liver, and its warming properties help to boost circulation. Can also ease menstrual pain and help with skin problems and minor wounds.

Yellow Rice
Turmeric is used to flavor and color rice. Cinnamon sticks, bay leaves, cardamom, and raisins are sometimes included.

Turmeric Spice
The ground rhizomes produce a powder that contains, among other constituents, a yellow dye called "curcumin," and a volatile oil.

Rhizomes
The rhizomes, or tubers, are light brown outside and yellow-orange inside, with a characteristic smell and taste.

Rhizomes
Pointed rhizomes are up to 3 in. long.

Seeds
Small, light brown seeds are used to propagate the plant.

Leaf
Narrow, dark green, branching leaflets have a scent similar to horseradish.

Stem
Round, green stems. True valerian stems have deep grooves running along them, distinctly different from other species of valerian.

Root
Valerian grows from a short rhizome with a mat of fibrous roots that smell unpleasant.

VALERIAN

Valerian has a long history in treating hysteria—it was used to treat shell shock in the trenches during World War I—since it has a tranquillizing effect. It is also an attractive garden plant.

True valerian is one of the most powerful herbal remedies available for an overwrought or stressed nervous system. It can be used for chronic or severe conditions where the whole system needs to be relaxed. Valerian was widely used to treat shell shock during World War I.

Medical herbalists use it very successfully in the treatment of hysteria and severe insomnia, as well as for reducing high blood pressure. Valerian has a painkilling, tranquilizing effect and is mildly narcotic. Its name comes from the Latin *valere,* "to be well," although it was also named *phu* by the Greek physician Galen—rather appropriately since its smell is unpleasant. True valerian has a round, hollow stem with grooves running down it. These help to distinguish it from other types of valerian. The plant has not been used much for culinary purposes, although four hundred years ago, it was said that poor people in northern England considered it a delicious flavoring for soups.

Ornamental Plant
Valerian's clusters of tiny, pale pink flowers appear in midsummer. Because of its height, it is best planted at the back of an herb border. Make sure that it cannot be damaged by cats—the smell attracts them, and they roll on damaged plants as if intoxicated! Witches called the plant "cat's paw."

If valerian is being grown ornamentally, it is not necessary to cut it back. But when it is grown for medicinal purposes, the flowers should be cut so that the plant's energy is diverted to the root. The roots can then be unearthed during late autumn, cleaned, and dried in the shade.

USES

PARTS USED:
Rhizomes.

PROPERTIES:
Bitter, warming, and sedative herb; relaxes spasms, calms nerves, relieves pain, aids digestion, and lowers blood pressure.

USES OF THE HERB:
Medicinal
Drink an infusion for painful periods or to ease shock. Take in the short term for insomnia.

Cosmetic
Use a decoction in soothing baths or as a facial wash to ease acne, skin rashes, or, occasionally, eczema.

Household
Valerian attracts cats and earthworms. Place the root of valerian in a mousetrap to catch vermin.

CAUTION
Do not take in conjunction with sedatives or sleep-inducing drugs, or for more than two weeks without a lengthy break. Valerian is a very powerful herb, and in too high a dosage, it can cause hallucination, headaches, giddiness, and agitation.

VANILLA

The pods of this plant, which is a type of orchid, provide the unmistakable taste and aroma of vanilla, probably the most widely used flavoring ingredient in the world.

The plant *Vanilla planifolia* gives its name to one of the world's most popular flavorings. It is actually a climbing orchid, native to tropical North, Central, and South America. The fruits of this orchid—also called pods or beans—are the important parts of this valuable commercial crop. Out of over one hundred different vanilla orchids, this species produces almost all of the famous aromatic extract. It is also the only orchid commercially cultivated for its practical, rather than decorative, value.

Vanilla pod extract contains varying amounts of the aromatic substance vanillin and has a distinctive sweet flavor used in all kinds of baked goods, desserts, ice creams, and drinks. It is also added to perfumes. Medicinally, vanilla extract can help to ease digestion.

Spanish Discovery
Vanilla was discovered by the Spanish conquistadores, who found it growing in Aztec Mexico—contemporary records mention it being used in chocolate. In the 1800s, a widespread craze for ice cream took off, and vanilla really came into its own.

Natural versus Imitation
There are various imitation and synthetic essences, some of which are made from the by-products of wood pulp. Real vanilla has a subtler quality and contains a complex mix of substances. Pure, high-quality extract should improve with age and should not have any sugar added.

Cultivation conditions must be shady, hot, and moist. The flowers are very carefully hand-pollinated at a certain time in the growth cycle, and the pods produced are handpicked about six months later, when they are fully ripe but before they split open. The green pods are then soaked, sun-dried, and fermented—a six-month process that turns them a blackish-brown color. The best beans are plump and flexible with better-quality or higher amounts of vanillin. Pods stay fresh for six months in refrigerated, sealed containers, while good essence lasts indefinitely and should even improve over a period of time.

Fruit
Long, thin, seed-containing capsules are dried to provide extracts used for flavoring and for scenting perfumes.

Leaf
Long, thick, fleshy, oblong leaves.

Ice Cream
Vanilla came into its own in the nineteenth century when ice cream became popular. A good-quality vanilla ice cream contains powdered vanilla, which tastes superior to those made with synthetic flavorings.

Dried pods
The pods are dried and fermented, turning them black, so that the valuable aromatic compounds develop. These fermented pods are around 8 in. long.

USES

PARTS USED:
Fruits.

PROPERTIES:
Aromatic.

USES OF THE HERB:
Culinary
Used to flavor cakes and pastries, ice creams, desserts, candy, syrups, sauces, and soft drinks. Adds an unusual note to seafood, soups, and vegetable stir-fries. A pod can also be stored in the sugar jar to give the sugar a vanilla flavor, or the seeds left in cottage cheese and yogurt for some hours. Pods used whole can be rinsed, dried, and used again.

Medicinal
Although rarely used medicinally, vanilla can be an effective aid to digestion.

WINTERGREEN

Leaf
Thick, shiny, leathery texture. Oval and dark green above, paler beneath. Toothed.

This creeping evergreen shrub was a traditional folk remedy for Native Americans. Its oil is still used for a range of conditions.

The leaves of this plant—and the oil extracted from them—have a long history of medicinal use stretching back well before the first European settlers arrived in North America. The oil contains methyl salicylate, a close relative of aspirin, and must be treated with care since it can cause liver and kidney damage and may be fatal in excess. It should never be taken by those who are hypersensitive to aspirin (salicylates).

Traditional Uses
Nowadays, oil of wintergreen has been largely replaced by synthetic compounds, but it was once a very important remedy for aches and pains, generally applied externally to treat rheumatism, arthritis, sciatica, myalgia, neuralgia, sprains, and so on. It also acts as a diuretic, antiseptic, and expectorant, and it is good for catarrh, and is said to improve milk flow in nursing mothers.

Woody Note
Aside from its healing powers, wintergreen is a well-known ingredient of perfumes, producing a rather woody note. Its leaves can be infused to make a tasty, therapeutic tea. The oil has economic value as a flavoring for root beer and toothpaste—usually combined with menthol and eucalyptus—and the berries were once steeped in brandy to make a bitter tonic. As these berries last throughout the winter, they provide a useful food source for wildlife such as birds and deer.

Household Remedy
The *Gaultheria* genus was named after Jean François Gaulthier, an eighteenth-century botanist and physician who worked in Canada. *Gaultheria procumbens* was particularly prized as an American household remedy in the nineteenth and early twentieth centuries, but had been a staple of native folk medicine well before that time. Nowadays, it is more likely to be cultivated to brighten up a winter rock garden or in a container. Makes good ground cover in moist peaty soil.

Fruit
Fleshy, aromatic, bright red berries ripen in autumn and last all winter.

Stem
Wiry branches.

USES

PARTS USED:
Leaves, oil.

PROPERTIES:
Aromatic, astringent, soothing, warming, diuretic, anti-inflammatory, expectorant, antiseptic.

USES OF THE HERB:
Medicinal
Oil of wintergreen contains methyl salicylate, similar in effect to aspirin. Applied externally for rheumatism, arthritis, sciatica, myalgia, sprains, neuralgia, and catarrh.

Culinary
Leaves infused for tea.

Cosmetic
Adds a woody note to perfume.

CAUTION
Oil of wintergreen should not be taken by those who are hypersensitive to aspirin (salicylates). It can damage the liver and kidneys and may be fatal in excess.

WITCH HAZEL

Distilled witch hazel is a common first-aid item in many home medicine cabinets because it is used for so many ailments.

Witch hazel is possibly the world's most popular astringent. Used to reduce inflammation, it is a common ingredient of eye drops, skin toners, and healing ointments. Distilled witch hazel is readily available over the counter for cosmetic or first-aid purposes—such as drying up acne and soothing insect bites or tired eyes. It is also applied to sprains, burns, bruises, sore nipples, nosebleeds, muscular aches, hemorrhoids, and varicose veins.

Mild Sedative
Witch hazel leaves, twigs, and bark have tonic and sedative properties, and are taken to check internal hemorrhaging and mucous discharge linked with conditions such as diarrhea, colitis, dysentery, hemorrhoids, vaginal discharge, heavy menstrual flow, bleeding in the stomach or lungs, or prolapsed organs. A sore throat mouthwash or gargle can be made by diluting one part distilled witch hazel with six parts water.

Dowser's Herb
The name "witch hazel" reflects a traditional belief in the plant's magical powers—its forked, hazel-like branches were once used as divining rods for water and gold. The Greek genus name *Hamamelis* translates as either "a pear-shaped fruit" or as *hama*—"at the same time"—and *melis*—"a fruit." This may refer to the fact that the flowers appear just as the previous year's black nuts are ripening. The tiny nuts contain edible seeds, which are suddenly and violently ejected from their shells, hence the alternative common name "snapping hazel."

Cultivation
Witch hazel is commercially cultivated for its economic value to the pharmaceutical and cosmetics industries. It is very hardy and prefers slightly acid, humus-rich soil.

USES

PARTS USED:
Leaves, branches, bark.

PROPERTIES:
Aromatic, astringent; checks bleeding and mucous discharge; reduces inflammation.

USES OF THE HERB:
Medicinal
Distilled witch hazel is a powerful astringent, anti-inflammatory, and handy remedy for acne, bites, burns, hemorrhoids, nosebleeds, varicose veins, sprains, bruises, muscular aches, and sore nipples. Dilute one part distilled witch hazel in six parts water for a mouthwash or gargle to soothe sore throats.

Cosmetic
Common ingredient of eye drops and skin-toning products.

CAUTION
Tincture of bark or leaves is not recommended for home use as it may disfigure skin.

Leaf
Oval with wavy edges—turn yellow in autumn.

Distilled Witch Hazel
Is included in many skin preparations for its astringent quality. It is also a handy home remedy for acne, nosebleeds, and insect bites.

Stem
Smooth gray bark.

Flower
Clusters of bright yellow, scented flowers bloom from late summer into autumn.

Flower
Numerous cross-shaped yellow blooms in early summer.

Leaf
Lanceolate (slender oval) foliage used for dye and medicinal preparations.

Stem
Branched, leafy stems.

Seeds
Long, hanging, purple-black seeds in large clusters.

WOAD

This plant has been used since ancient times to make a blue dye. It has also been used medicinally to treat a range of viral infections.

The blue woad pigment obtained from this plant, also called "dyer's weed," must be one of the best known dyes of all time—perhaps the first image conjured up is one of ancient Europeans using woad as a body paint. The Romans recounted tales of seeing Britons decorated with its dye. Pigment is produced by leaving crushed and partly dried leaves exposed to the air to form a powder.

The foliage and roots of this bitter, cooling biennial or perennial are also well known in herbal medicine. Extracts have been prescribed to counter a range of disease-causing organisms and to reduce inflammation and fever. Research suggests that woad remedies may also have a role to play in the fight against cancer.

Ancient History
Nowadays, this species is often found growing as a wild plant in cornfields and on cliff tops. The plant was widely cultivated for its pigment during ancient times and for many centuries afterward. Its days of massive cultivation for dying fabric waned after the 1600s, when indigo became more popular, but it is still grown intensively in some areas to produce certain black dyes and to improve the color of indigo. Fermenting woad plants to produce dye gives off a truly unpleasant smell—so much so that Elizabeth I forbade dye production near her palaces.

Bitter Medicine
During the 1930s, Mrs. Grieve, a leading herbal authority, suggested that internal medicinal use of this very bitter plant might be unwise due to its astringency and that it should be limited to external applications for ulcers and bleeding wounds. The Chinese, however, have taken the plant internally since at least the sixteenth century.

In the Garden
Woad is an especially interesting plant for the herb garden. Its bright yellow blooms, borne from late spring into summer, followed by attractive, shiny black seed heads, can make an attractive splash of color. It is easy to raise from seed, in situ, but plants in exposed positions may need staking as they form flower stems.

USES

PARTS USED:
Leaves, roots.

PROPERTIES:
Bitter, anti-inflammatory herb; lowers fever and may counter cancer.

USES OF THE HERB:
Medicinal
Found by many to be active against all kinds of infection, including viral disease, flu, and sore throats, thrush, meningitis, and mumps.

Household
Used for centuries as a blue dye.

CAUTION
A very bitter plant; may not be advisable to take internally.

YARROW

Often grown in gardens for its attractive foliage, this invasive plant has a long history. It is referred to in many myths and legends and has a range of medicinal uses.

Also known popularly as "soldier's woundwort," myth has it that Achilles used this common roadside weed to heal his troops' wounds after the famous siege of Troy—hence also the genus name of *Achillea*. The plant has been around for thousands of years and is associated with mythology and beliefs in many other parts of the world too—for example, stalks of yarrow are traditionally used when consulting the sacred Chinese book of wisdom, the *I Ching*.

Medicinal Uses

Medicinally, this is also a valued plant, and the whole dried herb is used to prepare a range of natural remedies. Yarrow is both bitter and astringent and contains an essential oil that reduces fever and inflammation, tackling conditions from flu to nosebleeds. Ayurvedic practitioners find it especially helpful for treating disorders of the nervous system. An infusion of fresh leaves and flowers makes a cleansing and toning addition to a bath.

Traditional Uses

Yarrow's reputation for controlling bleeding was handed down over many centuries—yet another common name was "staunchweed." The ancient Greeks revered its medicinal powers, as did the Anglo-Saxons, while others used it as an accompaniment to sorcery and magic rituals. It has been used by countless herbalists all over the world and was traditionally taken in the Scottish Orkney islands to banish melancholy.

Border Plant

It is invasive, so provided it is not allowed to get out of control, yarrow can make a good choice for a garden border. Its long, feathery, much-divided leaves—*millefolium*, or "a thousand leaves," refers to their many tiny segments—are delicately attractive, and the plant produces its long-lasting blooms from early summer through late autumn.

Flower
Dense, flat-topped heads of whitish, pink, or lilac blooms between summer and late autumn.

Leaf
Long and feathery; bottle green with peppery flavor.

Stem
Sturdy, upright, and furrowed. Branches toward the apex.

USES

PARTS USED:
Whole plant.

PROPERTIES:
Aromatic, astringent, bitter, diuretic herb; antispasmodic and anti-inflammatory, increases perspiration, relieves indigestion, lowers blood pressure, and helps to stop hemorrhage.

USES OF THE HERB:
Medicinal
Eases feverish illnesses (such as flu), high blood pressure, hemorrhage, indigestion, stomach cramps, diarrhea, menstrual problems, rheumatism, and arthritis; aids health of nervous system and may help to protect against thrombosis. External use helps to treat wounds, ulcers, nosebleeds, acne, and hemorrhoids.

Culinary
Leaves can be added to salads.

Cosmetic
Add a yarrow infusion to bathwater.

CAUTION
Must not take if pregnant; excess use may cause skin allergy or sensitize skin to sunlight.

INDEX (by Latin name)